AF439214

I CAN!
D.R.E.A.M.

5 Simple Steps to Your Success, Freedom, and Happiness

I Can! D.R.E.A.M.
Copyright © 2026 by Ron Carstens
All rights reserved.

No part of this publication may be reproduced, distributed, or transmitted in any form or by any means, including photocopying, recording, or other electronic or mechanical methods, without the prior written permission of the publisher, except in the case of brief quotations embodied in critical reviews and certain other noncommercial uses permitted by copyright law.

ISBN (paperback): 979-8-9939182-0-4
ISBN (ebook): 979-8-9939182-1-1

Book design and production by www.AuthorSuccess.com

Printed in the United States of America

I CAN! D.R.E.A.M.

5 Simple Steps to Your Success, Freedom, and Happiness

Transform Your Life from Ordinary to Extraordinary with the Newest Goal-Setting and Goal-Achievement Method

RON CARSTENS

Contents

Foreword

BY RUBEN GONZALEZ, FOUR-TIME OLYMPIAN

As a four-time Olympic athlete and entrepreneur, I know the importance and value of having a plan to reach your goals, the many challenges one can face, and the importance of other people's support. More importantly, I know you need a winning attitude and belief in yourself to reach those goals. These are established elements of success.

What Ron does in *I CAN! D.R.E.A.M.* is take these elements of success and breaks them down into easy steps for you to follow. You will learn proven goal-achievement techniques and apply them using a new, updated method that also considers your uniqueness.

Tackling goals can be intimidating, which often leads people not to even try or to quit when the going gets tough. Ron recognizes that people, regardless of their situation, face problems and sometimes need motivation and self-confidence. The new D.R.E.A.M. method shows you how to break down big goals into smaller tasks, build more motivation and confidence, and overcome a variety of challenges.

Ron genuinely cares about people and wants to help them live better lives. From students to experienced professionals, *I CAN! D.R.E.A.M.* is the help you need to achieve your goals and change your life.

So take action. Read and apply the lessons in *I CAN! D.R.E.A.M.*, and you'll be amazed at what you can accomplish.

Ruben Gonzalez
Four-Time Olympian, Bestselling Author, Keynote Speaker
TheLugeMan.com

Introduction

If I can **help you** avoid making a decision that will cost you $320,000 or more and **three years** of your life, would you want to hear what I have to say? Hopefully, that is a "Captain Obvious" answer. However, we sometimes make decisions, big and small, without knowing all the facts about a situation or without considering all the consequences, and those decisions can have a profound impact on our **lives**. And I, like many people, made one of those decisions that had the above consequences. Yes, sad face emoji.

DREAMING WITHOUT A D.R.E.A.M.

It was 1999. Although my government job was relatively stable, it was not a high-paying position. My coworker brought the daily newspaper to work, so, of course, I looked at it too. For the younger readers, yes, the newspaper with the big, folded pieces of paper, like you see in "old" TV shows and movies. The paper had an Employment section where businesses advertised job openings. Looking through the paper, I saw job postings where people with a college degree, which I had, and five years of work experience, which I had, were being offered salaries that were two or three times as much as my salary.

My thoughts were that I was a professional, and I, and others in my profession should get paid more, but that wasn't happening. I wasn't greedy; I only **wanted** to earn just a **little more money** to make a **better life** for myself and my family. Have you ever felt or thought that you should make more money? That you weren't being properly compensated for your hard work? Does this situation sound familiar to you? Many of you know exactly what I'm talking about.

Well, I decided to do something about it. I took action and changed to a completely different profession and employer. I became a financial advisor, concentrating on financial planning for individuals and small businesses, and at one point managed over $30 million in assets while working for a large, national bank. As a financial advisor, my income was 100% based on commissions, which gave me the potential to make a lot more money, but that also included more uncertainties and more risks.

In the beginning, the stock market was doing well, so selling was easy. Then, in less than two years, a series of tragic events took place that changed the financial industry and our country forever. First, the dot-com bubble burst. Then, the Worldcom and Enron bankruptcies occurred, followed by many other businesses' accounting scandals. Finally, there were the **September 11, 2001**, attacks on America.

These events had **devastating effects** across our society, especially on the financial industry and my job. My income went from somewhat predictable to completely uncertain, as customer confidence in the stock market was totally destroyed.

After 9/11, my customers wanted to sell everything and bury their money in their backyards. Seriously! That's what they told me. They sure as hell didn't want to give me more money to invest, which meant no commissions and no income for me. Those **uncertainties** and **risks** that came with my new career **came to a head** in a tidal wave of change no one could have predicted, marking the the beginning of the end of my new career. At the time, my **family needed** more **stability**, so after almost three years of adventure, I returned to my reliable government job and a steady paycheck, also known as **the comfort zone**.

LIKE MANY OF YOU

I, like many of you, just wanted a little more out of life. A better job, a nicer vacation, a newer car, to live in a little better neighborhood, to not have to work fifty to sixty hours a week, and to spend more time with my kids. We all **have dreams and goals,** yet **we fear** even saying them out loud**.** We are afraid of what other people will say or think about us, like we are being silly, or stupid, or not being realistic, or that we are just dreaming.

Even if we did acknowledge our dreams and desires**,** we still **didn't know how** to go about achieving them. We **weren't taught** in school, or at home, how to **set goals,** yet it is an **essential** and **helpful life skill**, and can make a a **huge difference** in our lives. We were taught, or rather told, to go to college and then get a job. We certainly weren't taught to **write** down our **goals** and set a specific timeframe for achieving them**,** or how to make an **action plan.** We simply didn't have the knowledge.

THE CONSEQUENCES

The most common consequence of this lack of knowledge is that we **don't take action**. Then five years pass, then ten, then fifteen years, and we still have the same desires and goals**.** And more often than not, we don't do anything about it except keep dreaming. We want a different future, but we don't know how to achieve it, so we **continue** living in our **status quo** of not setting and achieving goals.

Another consequence is that you **take action without a plan**, or you only have a limited plan, like my career change. My plan was to transition to a job with a significantly higher income potential, but I didn't have specific plans after that. Also, my goal to make more money was not clearly defined, which was also a huge mistake. While I had the motivation and courage to pursue my goal and make big changes in my life, I lacked the knowledge and a detailed plan as to the best way to reach my goal, which resulted in a **loss of my time** and **money**.

LESSONS LEARNED

Several years ago, when I started writing this book, I did an analysis of the consequences of my career change decision, and the results were a little shocking (and not in a good way). Due to the new pay raises I would have received in my old job and the nearly three years of time I missed in the pension plan, I calculated my actual financial loss to be just **over $220,000**. In addition, given that I could have been promoted at my first job during that time and taken advantage of a few other work-related benefits to increase my income, my **potential** financial **gains** were easily **over $100,000**. Hence, the **$320,000 loss** previously mentioned, which I consider a mistake, or at least an **unnecessary** and **expensive education.**

Are you thinking, *Well, that sucks?* I was. However, during those three years and since, I have been committed to self-improvement. I **learned** many new **skills** and **gained knowledge** and **experience.** Fortunately, I was, and am currently, able to put those skills to use. The experience has benefited me in many ways, giving me insight and **wisdom** that one only gets from living life, having goals, taking risks, failing, and learning from those experiences, which I'm now passing on to you.

YOU'RE NOT ALONE

Through the years, in talking with numerous people, I found that my **experience** was **not unique**. Many people had changed jobs or careers that didn't turn out as they'd hoped. These people also wanted just a little more in life, but they didn't know the best way to reach their goals. These **people** were also **looking for answers** as to how and what they should have done to achieve their desired outcomes of just a little more in life. I have also discovered these same thoughts in many young people. They weren't taught about goal setting and goal achievement either.

With **so much information** available in books, articles, programs, and advice on everything at your fingertips, it can leave one wondering **where to begin.** There are thousands of information sources on the subjects of success, goals, and goal achievement, but how do you know what advice or information is correct, or truthful, and **what information** is **right for you**? Again, you have a goal, but you don't know where to start, or which way to go next. It is a common problem for so many people.

THE SOLUTION: THE D.R.E.A.M. METHOD

To solve this problem, I took my 35-plus years of adult experience in life, in personal growth, and all the information I have consumed from a wide variety of sources on self-improvement, self-development, leadership, management, team building, training, goal setting, and goal achievement, and developed a **new goal-setting and goal-achievement method to help people achieve their goals.**

Now, **you** can **benefit** from my experience and education. I traveled down those long, bumpy roads that you don't need to go on unless you just want to learn things the hard way. And I did things the hard way when I didn't have to because, like most men, I don't like to stop and ask for directions. I often didn't have a real plan, follow a map, or have someone to guide me. I just started taking action and consequently wasted a lot of time, money, and energy (physical and emotional). Now, you can **avoid** all the **mistakes** and bad decisions that I made that led you to somewhere other than your goal.

Instead, you can **learn a new skill** and a new **system/method** for **goal setting and goal achievement**. After reading this book and **learning** the **D.R.E.A.M. Method,** you will know how to:

- **Develop** and **set goals**
- **Make** a list of steps (**action plan**) to reach your goal
- **Monitor** your goal **progress** and make adjustments
- **Avoid wasting time, energy, money**, or any other resource

You can achieve your dreams and goals, and have the life you want, with a lower risk of wasting resources. **Learning** and **applying** the **D.R.E.A.M. Method** is your **shortcut to success**.

My **purpose** is to **help you,** to show you how to make a **better life** for yourself and live the life you want by believing in yourself, setting goals, making a plan, and taking action, so you can **ACHIEVE YOUR GOALS** and **avoid** costly **mistakes**.

So please read on to live the life you are dreaming of.

CHAPTER 1
Why Goals Matter

*Setting goals is the first step in turning
the invisible into the visible.*

– Tony Robbins

Life is either a daring adventure or nothing.

– Helen Keller

THE FARMER WHO CHANGED THE WORLD

Have you heard of Henry Ford? Yes, as in Ford cars. Of course, you have. **Henry** Ford was the founder and creator of the Ford Motor Company. At age 12, while riding in a horse-drawn wagon, he saw a road engine, which was a large steam engine on wheels, and it was the first vehicle other than a horse-drawn one that he had seen. From that day forward, Ford had an interest in making a machine that would travel on roads. Ford felt farm life was hard work, too hard, and that motivated him to devise ways to do things better.

Later on in his life, Ford envisioned everyone owning a car. That was his dream/goal, but cars were expensive to make. **His goal** became **making cars affordable** so anyone, especially the working-class person, could buy one. While he didn't invent the first car, he was an early pioneer of automobiles, and **his inventions** and creations, like the **assembly line, revolutionized** and **changed the World**.

In pursuit of his goals, Ford pioneered:

- The Quadricycle, a small, gas-powered carriage that was a precursor to the Model T.

- The 40-hour work week in place of the 60- to 70-hour work week.

- Weekends off instead of just one day off.

- The assembly line, which revolutionized production and changed the World.

- And the Model T, an affordable and reliable car.

Today, the Ford Motor Company has produced around 400 million cars, and the name "Ford" is known worldwide. That's pretty amazing, considering Henry Ford started life as a farm boy and had limited formal education. Despite his lack of formal education and money, he became an **inventor**, a creator of technology, a trailblazer, a **World leader** in the automobile industry, and one of the **richest** men in America.

And it all started with a child's dreams. A **12-year old's imagination and thoughts** about vehicles that weren't even invented yet **changed the World**.

A COMMON SITUATION

However, for most people, their lives just happen. Morning comes, and you get up and go to work, or school, or take care of the kids, or all the above. Later, you come home and think, I should exercise, or call my friend, or do this thing or that thing. However, you are tired and not quite ready to do that thing yet, and you procrastinate. Then, you read emails, eat dinner, watch some TV or Netflix, scroll some or lots of social media, and before you know it, the day is gone. As you get ready for bed, you think to yourself about all the things you should have done, but oh well, **I will do that tomorrow**, time for bed. Does this sound familiar?

Then, tomorrow comes and **you repeat** the **same day**. Sadly, this same day turns into weeks, months, years, and sometimes lifetimes. The proof is in your, my, and countless people's unattained goals, dreams, or desires. The proof is your regrets about things you never did, or about things you put off for a long time.

Dr. David Kohl, a highly regarded former professor and academic Hall of Famer in the College of Agriculture at Virginia Tech, Blacksburg, Va., highlights people's lack of goals and lack of writing them down in a 2024 article of his that states:

- **80%** of people **do not have any goals**.

- **16%** have **goals, but** they are **not written down**.

- Only **4% write** their **goals** down.

And the **big eye-opener** from Dr. Kohl:

- **People who regularly write their goals down earn nine times as much** over their lifetimes than people who don't.

This last finding about lifetime earnings should be enough motivation for everyone to write their goals down.

AVERAGE RESULTS

However, the reality is most **people DO NOT** consciously choose to **set goals** or **not set goals**. We all have dreams, desires, and wants, but no one taught us to have high expectations, set goals, or how to achieve them.

Rather, we were **taught** to **act** and **think like others.** Our society taught us to **conform** to its established norms. We've all heard sayings like, *just follow the crowd, go with the flow, go along to get along, don't rock the boat, don't be greedy, and go to college and then get a good job.* We learned from our family, friends, school, and the media to **accept** the condition of things, people, and circumstances as they are, and the **way things are** for most people **is the average.**

If you are part of the **80%** of people with no goals, then you are getting **average results** in life, which are sometimes good, sometimes bad, and sometimes neutral. Essentially, **you are gambling** on the outcome of **your future** and getting **random results**.

That's how life works. **Life** considers all the circumstances, including your decisions that led you to where you are today, then, based on all of those circumstances, it **will choose** for you again, and again tomorrow, and the next day, and the next. And the typical results you get **when you don't choose** what you want in life are just that, typical or **average** results. Outstanding, great, or fantastic results in life require different choices and actions.

Are you happy with the results you've gotten so far in life? If you are, that's great, but would you like better results? If you had a choice of getting excellent results or average ones, which would you choose? Yes, another "Captain Obvious" moment, of course, you would choose the excellent results.

However, that's not what most people do. Again, **most people don't choose** at all. Unfortunately, not choosing to take action is still making a choice for the average. In short, **unless you** are actively **deciding** on the results you want in life **and taking action**, then **life chooses** the results **for you** and will continue to do so.

BETTER RESULTS

*** SECRET ***

You can change your results in life, and you CAN choose to have better results and a better life.

Yes, you read that correctly: you CAN change your results and achieve better-than-average outcomes in life. It only **requires you to set and achieve goals** and be honest with yourself, which can be hard sometimes, as we don't always like to accept certain truths about ourselves. However, some honest self-reflection can lead to discovering and acknowledging your true desires and goals.

Here are a few questions to help with your self-reflection and self-discovery:

- Do you have the life you want?
- What more do you want out of life?
- Do you feel stuck in a place, a mood, a job, or a relationship?
- Do you feel that you have "settled" for your current life?
- If so, what would you change?
- Do you say, I wish that I would have . . . ?

- If so, how would you finish that statement?
- How many things would be on your "wish you would have..." list?

Knowing your true desires and goals is important because it's these goals that you are more likely to act on. And it's those burning desires and **true goals** that **can** and will **transform you** and an average life into a **better you** and a **fantastic life** if you simply acknowledge and act upon them.

WHY SET GOALS?

*** SECRET ***

Simply put, **you should set goals so you get good results because life happens to you whether you want it to or not,** and you will continue to get more results whether you want them or not. Those results can be good, bad, or indifferent, but regardless, they are coming. And if you do not have any goals, then your results are going to be random and average. It's why goals matter.

An argument I've heard people make against setting goals and spending time planning them out is that you **can't control everything**. And they are right, you can't control everything that goes on around you, but you **can influence them**. Another argument I've heard is why should you bother setting goals if most people don't achieve them anyway?

I think most people, even pessimists, will accept as true that if they had a choice of getting excellent results in life or average ones, they would choose excellent results. Right? Of course. If you wouldn't choose excellent results, that's fine, but if you do, know you are not being greedy. You are being smart. There is **abundance** in this World, and it's okay to want more and get more, but you **must set goals** and **take action** to get those excellent results.

*** SECRET ***

By setting goals and taking action to reach them, YOU get to decide the outcomes of your life rather than life deciding for you, and you get better results.

Also, **setting goals** is an important **part of** personal development and **success**. Setting goals **helps** you to **decide and define what is important** to you and gives you a **sense of purpose and direction**. Having a clear **sense of purpose** in life is important for your overall well-being.

Other **benefits of setting goals** are that they help you:

- **Clarify your priorities**. By setting goals, you can decide what is most important to you and allocate your time and resources accordingly.

- **Stay motivated**. When you have something specific to work towards, it can be easier to stay motivated and overcome obstacles that may arise.

- **Improve your time-management skills**. When you set goals, you can break them down into smaller tasks and set deadlines for yourself. These practices help you manage your time more effectively and get more done.

- **Develop new skills**. By setting goals that require you to learn new skills or knowledge, you force yourself to grow and develop as a person.

In studies of **successful people**, on the lists of **characteristics** and **habits** of these people are **goal setting**, **working hard** toward their goals, and **persistence** in achieving their goals. It's not a secret formula that rich people have been hiding. In short, **set a goal, work hard** and/or **smart** for it, and **don't give up.** It's not rocket science. Unless, of course, your goal is to be a rocket scientist. Yes, that was humor.

Also, working hard is subjective and varies from person to person. Some entrepreneurs and leaders work long days, while others believe in working smarter, not harder or longer. However, the **work must be done;** that is the hard part, but with **persistence**, your goals become attainable.

And the **D.R.E.A.M. Goal-Setting and Goal-Achievement Method** will teach you this **success formula.** The **D.R.E.A.M. Method** will show and help you:

- **Decide what you** want and how to write your goals out.

- Determine **Resources** you have and need to achieve your goals.

- **Evaluate** your starting situation and determine the best way to reach your goal.

- Create an **Action plan** which is a list of steps needed to reach your goal.

- **Monitor** your progress and make adjustments if needed.

In summary, you should make goals and take action, so you get the outcomes or results in life that you want, not what life decides for you. Having goals is important because they help you grow as a person, stay motivated, and give you a sense of purpose. Whether you are setting personal or professional goals, it is important to take the time to think about what you want to achieve and create a plan to make them happen.

Without dreams and goals, there is no living, only merely existing, and that is not why we are here.

– Source Unknown

CHAPTER 2

You Can't Copy Someone Else's Homework

*The biggest adventure you can ever take
is to live the life of your dreams.*

– Oprah Winfrey

*If you cannot do great things yourself, remember
that you may do small things in a great way.*

– Napoleon Hill

YOUR GOALS, YOUR JOURNEY

At this point, you should know why setting goals is so important, and, hopefully, you have a few goals in mind. In the coming chapters, you will learn the new **D.R.E.A.M.** goal-setting and goal-achievement method. However, before you get started, I have a few words of wisdom. When it comes to goal achievement, you can't copy someone else's homework.

Accomplishing your goals is like following directions on a road-map or road app. Think Google Maps or Waze. First, you enter **your starting point,** and second, you enter **your destination**, a.k.a. your goal. Then, you're given directions, a list of steps to follow, to reach your destination. The **directions shown** on your phone are **specifically for you** and you alone.

For example, you and your friend live ten minutes away from each other and agree to meet at a restaurant halfway between you. You both look up the address on the internet and get directions. While you both drive at different speeds, durations, and distances, and take different turns, you both end up at the same place. That's because the instructions given to you for your path were custom-made just for you, based on your current situation, location, and the best route for you. Goal setting and goal achievement work the same way.

If your friend texted you their directions, those directions wouldn't work for you because you have a different starting location/ situation. However, that's what many people try to do. They want to copy someone else's work, take a shortcut, or find a hack. They don't want to do the work needed. As a result, they end up going in the wrong direction, and even for a short time or distance, it causes you to **waste resources** like time and money.

YOUR UNIQUENESS MATTERS

Your unique starting location, circumstances, and goal determine and affect the path or route you need to take toward your goal. A person's goal may not be unique, but their personal circumstances, experiences, and motivations are. These are some of the reasons **why** you have so many **varied outcomes** of successes and failures from people trying to achieve the same or similar goals.

Those varied outcomes interested me and motivated me to learn more about goal setting and goal achievement. It showed me that the path or **journey you follow** to your goals **needs** to be **designed for you**, not for someone else. The big, red mountain I'm climbing is not the same as yours, which is not the same as someone else's. Also, it's why you **shouldn't compare yourself** and your progress to other people, which is covered more in Chapter 10.

There are self-help/self-improvement programs that say all you have to do is model or copy a successful person's actions or behaviors, and you can get the same results as the successful person. However, life is not always that simple, and it takes more than just copying someone's actions to be successful. While **modeling** a successful person's actions is usually a **good hack**, you still need to **make certain** that the actions or behaviors you are copying are **appropriate** for your situation.

Furthermore, while you can model someone's behaviors or specific actions and produce a similar result, you **can't model** someone's exact **thoughts, experiences, or motivations**. It's those differences between individuals that have a huge impact on goal achievement, even if those individuals have the same goal. Therefore, you can't always expect to produce the same outcome. That's why you need to establish your own goals and plans to reach your goals. You **must walk your own path**, not someone else's, just as they can't walk on your path, even if you are both headed for the same or similar destinations.

MY JOURNEY

Some of **my life experiences** and my **journeys,** here at the the end of writing this book, are listed below. It shows the number of years I've spent being or doing a certain thing.

YEARS: BEING/DOING

56 years: on Earth

51: a friend (yes, I have a friend that I've known since I was five years old)

50: a student (learning should never stop)

41: in the workforce

41: a best friend

39: owning a car

36: teaching and training others

34: in law enforcement (field **trainer/evaluator, taught** new detectives)

26: not completely satisfied with my career

21: a father

19: married

18: a Veteran

14: officially Catholic, but 36 years going to Catholic Churches

10: divorced

8: in the military (Army-also **teaching**)

7: finding my purpose and doing something about it

5: getting my college degree

5: trying to have a child (100+ doctor visits, fertility treatments, 2 operations (ex-wife), $20k)

5: writing this book

4: helping my elderly parents

3: changing jobs/careers and working in the corporate world

3: over my goal to finish writing this book

1: substitute **teaching,** K-12

Most of the experiences and situations I have been through in my life are not exceptional. Some are more common than others, while some are less common, and some are even rare. My joining the Army, getting a college degree, becoming a police officer, and becoming a father were not unique experiences.

However, all my circumstances and experiences together give me my unique starting points and life journeys. You can't replicate them, and no one can replicate yours. There are too many factors involved, which is why **your goals** and **your journey** to achieve them **are** individually **unique** to you. And that's why, **You Can't Copy Someone Else's Work!** You have to **do** your **own**.

MY GOALS

I've always been passionate about writing, learning new things, and have always enjoyed teaching people. While in the Army, I taught classes on a variety of subjects. During my career changes, I worked as a substitute teacher for a short time because I had an interest in teaching and wanted that experience. With the police department, I was a field trainer and evaluator for several years, which meant that after cadets graduated from the police academy, I trained and evaluated them on how to be a Patrol Officer. Also, while in the Homicide Division, I helped train investigators new to the division on how to conduct investigations of homicides, officer-involved shootings, and kidnappings. And while working on my goal of being a great dad, I taught my sons about the importance of goals and experimented (humanely, of course) on them on how to set and achieve goals. Their results so far are that they have achieved most of the goals they set, or are still working on them.

For a long time, I considered my fondness for teaching as just a small part of me. I didn't view it in terms of who or what I was. However, in narrowing down what I believed was **my purpose** or **one of my purposes in life**, and looking at my **experience/ journey list**, I discovered that I have **been a teacher** for pretty much my entire adult life. And I truly enjoy it and want to continue teaching. It continues to be one of my goals.

YOUR JOURNEY

Your journey through life is also **unique**. No matter your age, you have a unique list of experiences. Go ahead and get out your goal folder, or start one, or go to the website icandream.net, under Resources and you'll have access to a downloadable form. Make an **Experience List** and see what it looks like. You can use the one in the Appendices section in the back of this book. You might be surprised at how long you have been doing certain things. Also, if you are looking for your purpose, your list may give you a hint as to your purpose(s) in life.

If you are a younger person, you may have a short list and not notice any trends and that's okay. You don't need to know your "life purpose" when you are young. Plus, you can have more than one purpose, and you can change them if you want. However, **focusing** and planning on **one purpose or goal** at a time will **give you better results**.

YOUR GOALS

It's been said that if you do what you love, then you will never work a day in your life. What are you passionate about? What are your goals/plans? It's time to **start thinking** about them. What would make you happy, or happier? What do you want **to Be, Do, Have, or Achieve** in life? **Where** do you want to go? **Who** do you want to do those things with?

Your plans or road maps to reach your goals will be unique. A generic, one-size-fits-all plan doesn't work. You **need plans specifically for you** and your goals, and that's what the **D.R.E.A.M. Method** will **teach you.** It's just **5 simple steps.**

YOUR CHOICES FOR SUCCESS

There are thousands of self-development books and programs on the subject of goals and goal-setting. Recently, I have seen some new programs and "hacks" that tell you to forget about goal setting. Instead, they are now telling/selling you that you need to change your paradigms, or change your belief systems, or change your subconscious.

Those programs are partially correct, in that for many people, their belief systems are keeping them from being successful. In those situations, a change is needed. Those belief-changing programs and hacks can overcome mental roadblocks, which will be discussed in Chapter 10: Don't Listen to The Haters: Overcoming Obstacles.

However, the **change** recommended by those gurus **is still a goal**, so it **doesn't make sense to stop goal-setting** and goal-achievement. Instead, you should **embrace** it. And the best way to achieve a change is to have a process or system to follow that shows you how to properly set a goal and develop a plan of action to achieve it. Your goals or changes just don't happen on their own. Consequently, you **must learn** and **continue to set** and **achieve goals,** and you will be **successful.**

THE BEST BOOK, PROGRAM, OR SYSTEM FOR YOU

What book, program, or system is the best? Hopefully, this book helps you. However, the answer is **the one that gets you to**

take action. We are all different, and our thought and learning processes work in different ways. What works for one person may not work for another. Also, we just connect better with some authors and speakers than others, which makes continuing to learn and exposing yourself to different material so important.

While some people know with certainty what they want to achieve, and have those goals and actions set in their mind, most people do not fit into that category. **Most people** fit into the "I **need a little help**" category. We need help **planning our goals** and **making an action plan** to achieve those goals. We aren't the high achievers that we would really like to be, but we're working on it.

Why not? The answer for most people is that we just **don't know how to get started**, or we are **unsure of** what the **best way** is to accomplish our goal. We let our various **fears** override our desire for our goals, and then, we do nothing. Unfortunately, that is the norm.

HOW DO YOU BEGIN YOUR GOAL JOURNEY?

You begin your goal achievement journey **by educating yourself** about your goals, conducting extensive research, and learning about goal setting and achievement. And the **I CAN! D.R.E.A.M. Goal-Setting and Goal-Achievement Method is a great place to start,** especially if you are new to goal setting and goal achievement. Read this book and apply the **D.R.E.A.M.** method and techniques and never give up on your goals.

Then **continue learning**, and read another book, or take a class, or complete a program on a topic that interests you. And repeat. **Learning should be a lifelong goal.** Educating yourself about your goals will help you identify which are most important to you and clarify them.

*** SECRET ***

You should begin your goal journey by educating yourself, and learning should be a lifelong goal.

But first, you need to prepare your mind and learn **The Absolute, Most Important Thing You Must Do.**

I always say the same thing—which is to read as much you possibly can. Nothing will help you as much as reading.
– J. K. Rowling

Never just follow the crowd. Make up your own mind what you want to do and, if necessary, get the crowd to follow you.
– Margaret Thatcher

CHAPTER 3

The Absolute, Most Important Thing You Must Do

Whether you believe you can do a thing or not, you are right.
– Henry Ford (mic drop)

You can do anything you decide to do.
– Amelia Earhart

THE MOST INFLUENTIAL WOMAN IN THE WORLD

Oprah Winfrey was born into poverty to a single mother who didn't have time to take care of her. She was so poor that she had to wear potato sacks for clothes. She was passed around to different family members for primary care and was sexually abused for years by several family members who were supposed to be taking care of her.

Despite the emotional and physical trauma she endured as a child, she showed a talent and passion for public speaking at an early age. Fortunately, her grandmother taught her to read at three years of age and she really enjoyed it. Her **reading** and **learning habits helped** her graduate high school a year early and get a college scholarship.

From there, Oprah's communication talent got her jobs in radio and TV, from local news to her own talk show. *The Oprah Winfrey Show* became the highest-rated daytime talk show in the nation, and **Oprah** became, and is still, a **household name.** Numerous organizations nominated her at least 100 times for awards, and she's won dozens of them, including Academy Awards, Emmys, Golden Globes, Tonys, and People's Choice Awards.

Oprah was the **first black American woman to own her own production company** and became a media and TV giant. She became the **second black, female billionaire** in the United States, and is **one** of the **wealthiest women** in the **World**. She's been named the **most influential woman** in **America,** the **most influential woman** in the **World,** and one of the **most influential** and **successful people** in the **World**.

Rejected to Rewarded

Have you heard of **J. K. Rowling?** Most people have heard of J. K. Rowling, the author of the popular Harry Potter series. She has **sold over 500 million** copies of those books, and the Harry Potter movies are one of the highest-grossing movie franchises of all time. Did you know **12 publishers rejected** her before one finally accepted her first book?

Have you heard of **Jack Canfield?** Maybe a few of you recognize the name Jack Canfield, but most do not. Jack Canfield is a

non-fiction writer, and rather than his name, people remember his book titles, the ***Chicken Soup for the Soul*** series, which has also **sold over 500 million copies**. However, his first book in his *Chicken Soup for the Soul* series was **rejected by 144** publishers before one accepted it. 144! That's a lot of rejection.

Now, he's one of the **highest-selling** non-fiction **authors** in the **World.** He has had **47 books** on the *New York Times* **Bestseller** list and **set a record** for having **seven books** on the *New York Times* **Bestseller** list, at the **same time.** And he is recognized as one of the **leading success coaches.**

What Made These People Successful?

How does someone go from poor to one of the wealthiest people in the World? From a traumatized child to one of the Most Influential People in the World? From a secretary and rejected writer, to a billionaire, having one of the most popular book series and movie franchises in history? From a schoolteacher and severely rejected writer, to a record-setting bestselling author and success coach?

There are thousands of **success stories** just like these **from people** just **like You.** People who didn't start life out as successful, but **they became successful.** So, what made these people and others successful?

They were successful because **they believed in themselves.** They **did not let** their current circumstances, race, gender, social status, financial status, or any other **circumstances limit them.** And they **took action. Your race, age, gender, religion, social or economic status, disability, experience, or other circumstance does not matter.** I suggest you read that last sentence again, or 20 times, or at least until you believe it. All those factors only tell you what your starting situation is; they do not determine your success.

*** **SECRET** ***

Your success will be determined by your self-belief and your actions.

Self-Belief refers to an individual's belief, trust, or confidence in their own abilities, judgments, and qualities. It encompasses a broad range of thoughts and attitudes, such as self-esteem and self-confidence.

Similar but different, **Self-esteem** is an individual's overall sense of self-worth and the **value** they place **on themselves,** while **Self-confidence** is an individual's belief in their **ability to succeed** in **specific situations** or accomplish certain tasks.

Why Do You Need to Know About Self-belief?

Unfortunately, many **people** have **experienced** a lifetime of **negative reinforcement.** The limiting beliefs of others got passed on to them, and the result is low self-belief and continued limiting behavior and actions.

What do I mean? Have you ever dreamed about being famous, maybe a pro athlete, a musician, a doctor, or some other highly skilled job or popular occupation? Then, you told someone your dream, and they said, *that's silly, or, that's crazy, or don't get your hopes up, or why don't you just be a "fill-in-the-blank here"* with something that is not your dream. Instead of encouraging you to go after your dreams and take big actions or risks to achieve your goals, **those people, the haters, suggest you change your goal** to something smaller, easier, safer, something they think you can do, or something that limits your desired ideas.

While those people may not intend to limit your beliefs, or give you negative feedback, or negative reinforcement, that's exactly what they do. And when you get negative feedback from a friend or family member, especially over and over, that negative feedback often results in limiting your behavior. **Their limiting beliefs become your limiting beliefs,** which results in your not taking action to reach your dreams or goals. You limit your behavior and take small steps instead of big ones. You turn your big dreams and ideas into smaller ones, and **the result** is you live an **average life**, or worse, a **life** filled **with regrets**. Regrets of unfulfilled dreams.

Boosting your **self-belief helps** you **avoid regrets** and **positively impacts your self-esteem, self-image, motivation**, and your **ability** to **accomplish goals**. When people have faith in themselves and their capabilities, they are more likely to **embrace challenges**, persist in the face of setbacks, and ultimately achieve their goals. Also, a strong sense of self-belief can lead to **better decision-making.** The benefits of self-belief are some of the reasons that motivated me to write this book. It's because self-belief is so important, and you **can develop and improve it**.

THE MOST IMPORTANT THING

In fact, **self-belief** is the **foundation** for **personal achievement.** It's the basis or **starting point** for **achieving** your goals. It is the **first rock** you place when **building** a **better you**.

And the **Absolute, Most Important Thing You Must do**, to:

- start your personal growth
- accomplish any goal you set

- make your dreams come true

- transform you and your life for the better

is, You Must Think and Believe: <u>I CAN!</u>

With total conviction of your mind, body, and soul, You Must Think and Believe,
    <u>I CAN</u> BE! <u>I CAN</u> DO! <u>I CAN</u> HAVE! <u>I CAN</u> ACHIEVE!–
any of my goals.

***** SECRET *****

For your success, the Absolute, Most Important Thing You Must Do is THINK and BELIEVE: I CAN!

Your I Can! mindset and belief in yourself is the most important message in this book, or any self-development, personal growth, or self-improvement book or program. Period! And no, I'm not overstating it. It is that important. It is the starting point for any goal and success.

If you truly **believe** that **you can** accomplish any goal that you desire to accomplish, and you **persist in your actions** toward that goal, then **you can achieve it.** Even if **you don't know exactly how** you are going to accomplish your goal, you must, and should, believe that your goals and dreams are possible and that you can make them happen. You **need** to have the **belief and attitude of I CAN!**

I can be . . . a best-selling author, engineer, business owner, musician, teacher, professional athlete, great mom or dad.

I can have a . . . seven-bedroom house with a pool, Porsche Boxster Spyder, vacation house on the beach, and six kids.

I can do/achieve . . . **climb that big red mountain**, get a doctorate degree, start my own business, work as a volunteer, learn a new language, travel the world, or have lunch with Jack Canfield. (Don't laugh, it's one of my goals)

Your **"I CAN" belief,** combined with **persistent action,** is the **key** to your success in **achieving** your **goals** and **transforming your life**. Also, it's the starting point for changing your belief systems and habits.

The Negative Side: I Can't

If you start with the thought or belief of "I can't," and you think that you can't do something, well, guess what, you are certainly more likely to fail at it. A lack of self-belief or self-confidence can have many **adverse effects** on an individual and their chances at success.

When individuals lack confidence in themselves, it may cause them to:

- underestimate their abilities

- avoid taking necessary risks

- avoid trying new things

- not take on new challenges or opportunities

- not overcome challenges.

These missed opportunities could have been opportunities that led to your personal growth, your desires and goals coming true. Hence, why it's so important to **be mindful** of any **limiting beliefs** and **doubts, especially, "I can't."**

Chapter 10 will address overcoming limiting beliefs and other obstacles, as these things will occur. Obstacles and difficulties are just a part of life. They are going to happen. How you respond to them will determine if you are successful or not.

DREAM Big!

The few example goals listed previously, like becoming a doctor or having a big house, are what I would call normal or reasonable goals. I want you to know that your, **I Can!** belief **applies** to **big, awesome**, and **"impossible" goals** as well.

One question that Success, Life, or Performance coaches often ask is, "If you knew you couldn't fail at something, what is it that you would do?" They ask that question because the answer is usually something that is important to you and probably a dream or desire you have. However, you often consider that dream/desire/goal to be too big, or you have some sort of mental obstacle that stops you from trying.

If you think one of your goals is too big, consider Elon Musk's goals of interplanetary colonization and integration of Artificial Intelligence with humans. Or Jeff Bezos' company, Blue Origin, whose mission is to make space travel more accessible and affordable.

Some people would say or think that colonization of another planet, probably Mars, is impossible or crazy. Crazy, kind of, since Mars does not have a breathable atmosphere, but impossible? NO! We've already had people living in the International Space Station for months at a time. Also, consider what Musk has already accomplished. He launched a rocket that went into space, flew back, and did a controlled landing with it. He's sent several spacecraft to the International Space Station, and he's had a commercial flight into space. Blue Origin has had multiple suborbital flights for paying customers.

You might think, "Well, they are billionaires, so they can do those sorts of things." My response is, they didn't start off as billionaires, and they didn't accomplish all those things until they set them as goals.

Your mind can conceive all sorts of fantastic ideas and thoughts. Some of those ideas may seem crazy to other people, and maybe even you. However, if you believe they are possible, then you can achieve them. Remember the first quote at the beginning of this chapter and focus on it: **if you believe you can . . . or cannot, you are right!**

Azim Premji, a billionaire business owner, said, "If people aren't laughing at your goals, your goals are too small." So **don't limit yourself, don't let other people limit you**, and never think your dream or goal is too big or impossible.

There are many books just about believing in yourself and not limiting yourself. I could go on and on with unique examples of how so many people limit themselves and reasons they shouldn't and why you shouldn't, but I'm hoping you get the point. The **key** is to **believe You Can!**

In Chapter 11: Tips, Hacks and Advanced Planning, you will find techniques to build up your I Can! belief and attitude. However, for now, just know you are smart enough, you are good enough, you are worthy of, and you deserve success and happiness.

The following question is a reality check for you: **Do you** have the courage to **believe you can achieve** your **goals?** If so, then **say it** out loud. **NOW!** If you yelled out "YES!" that's outstanding, and you're on your way to success. If you didn't, then hopefully you will by the end of the book.

Whatever the mind can conceive and believe, it can achieve.

– Napoleon Hill

CHAPTER 4

The D.R.E.A.M.
Goal-Setting and
Goal-Achievement Method

*Goals are about the results you want to achieve. Systems
are about the processes that lead to those results.*

– Atomic Habits, James Clear

Success leaves clues.

– Tony Robbins

THE D.R.E.A.M. METHOD

So now that you have your **I CAN!** belief and attitude, it's time to learn the **D.R.E.A.M. Goal-Setting and Goal-Achievement Method**. The **D.R.E.A.M. Method** is a **new system** for you to follow that **helps you reach a goal.** It's a **step-by-step process** that shows you how to develop and **decide** on your goals, how to make an **action plan** of the steps/actions needed to reach your goal, and how to **monitor** your progress and make course corrections when needed. This chapter briefly explains the method, and the following chapters on each step will explain them in greater detail.

D.R.E.A.M. stands for:

<u>D</u> Decide:

Decide what you want, in detail, by when. What is your goal? What do you want to have, be, do, or achieve? Describe your goal in detail. And by what date do you want to complete it?

<u>R</u> Resources:

What Resources do you have and what resources do you need? Resources can be tangible things like money or people with certain skills, or intangible things like your credit score or skills you want/ need to develop.

<u>E</u> Evaluate:

You need to Evaluate your starting situation and know where you are starting from, so you can determine the best route to reach your goal. Your starting situation is all the factors that affect your goal or your ability to reach your goal, like your resources. Also, what obstacles do you have or foresee?

<u>A</u> Action Plan:

Write an action plan with specific tasks, activities, or steps to accomplish your goal, including timeframes.

<u>M</u> Monitor:

Monitor your progress by keeping track of tasks, activities, or steps completed that you established in your Action Plan and measuring their outcomes. You also consider new circumstances or obstacles that arise, like a specific task that had to be delayed for a week. **Considering** your progress and results, and any new circumstances or information, then you decide if you need to change your Action Plan, and if so, you make those course corrections.

The D.R.E.A.M. Method is your route to goal achievement. Just like following directions to a location on a map, you simply follow the steps of the **D.R.E.A.M. Method,** and you get to where you want to be. However, unlike map directions that you follow, the **DREAM Method teaches** you how to **create** your **own directions** to follow, your **own steps** to achieving your goal. It provides you with a route to accomplish any of your goals in just **5 simple steps.**

An example of the D.R.E.A.M. Method:

Step 1: Decide

My goal is to weigh 190 lbs. by September 1, 2025.

Step 2: Resources

Have	**Need**
Weights	A weekly exercise plan
Row machine	A weekly diet plan
Bicycle	
Internet-can research any resources you need	

Fitness coach/accountability partner

And a pair of tennis shoes

Step 3: Evaluate

My **Starting Situation** is that I currently weigh 210 lbs. Based on my schedule, I have free time in the late afternoons and can exercise for 30-60 minutes. Meal prep on Sunday. Will do internet research and come up with a weekly meal plan. Will get an exercise plan from my fitness coach.

Step 4: Action Plan: Week 1

Day 1	**Day 2**	**Day 3**	**Day 4**	**Day 5**	**Day 6**	**Day 7**
Weights-✓	Row-✓	Weights-✓	Walk	Weights-✓	Bike	Recover
arms/legs		chest/legs		back/legs		Reward
Healthy meals	✓✓	✓✓	✓✓✓	✓✓✓	✓✓	Meal prep

Put check marks next to completed activities, and for each daily, healthy meal.

Step 5: Monitor

Weekly measurements: 1. Days of exercise- four

2. Days w/two healthy meals- five

3. Weight-lost 2 lbs., weighed 208 lbs.

For Action Plan: Week 2 and the following weeks, you can repeat the prior week or change around the type of workouts, times, etc., to suit your preferences, needs, and goal.

Week 2: Monitor: Had the flu and couldn't work out. Only ate two meals/day. Weight stayed at 208 lbs. Course Correction-repeat Week 2. If you got sick the week before your goal due date, then you may need to extend your goal another week. If so, it is no big deal, just make another weekly Action Plan and take action.

Why D.R.E.A.M.

Most people who have studied personal growth have heard of S.M.A.R.T. goals. It was one of the goal-setting methods I first learned. The acronym first appeared in the November 1981 issue of Management Review, in an article titled "There's a S.M.A.R.T. way to write management's goals and objectives," written by George T. Doran. It was created to help management develop goals with employees for more productive results in the workplace. The **original S.M.A.R.T.** acronym stood for **Specific, Measurable, Assignable, Realistic,** and **Time-related.**

Since then, **people** have **changed** the **acronym** for individual use and adapted it for their own purposes. Various sources that used the acronym also changed the meaning of one or more of the letters. Typically, the "S" for "Specific" stayed the same, but I found changes to all the other letters. As a result, they **changed** the **method.**

Changes I found included the "M" to represent **Motivational** instead of Measurable. The "A" changed to mean **Achievable, Accountable, Attainable, Aligned,** and **Action-oriented.** The "R" changed to **Relevant** or **Related.** And the "T" changed to **Time specific,** which is at least close to the original, but I also found it changed to **Trackable** in another source.

All these **different versions** and explanations only created **redundancy** and a **lack of clarity** in the method. While most of the changes were only slightly different, the various versions could create different plans and outcomes for the same goal.

Also, a **big problem** for me was/is that I didn't like the terms **Realistic, Relevant, or Achievable.** Those terms can be **very subjective** and can be **limiting beliefs.** I understand wanting to make Realistic goals for people in an organization, as you don't want to set people up for failure. However, applying it to an individual's goal can be even more subjective and limiting.

My goal is to teach people a method or system on how to set and achieve goals. I want people to have an **I Can!** attitude, and **plan** for and **achieve big goals** as well as small ones. But I will not teach a limiting goal-setting method that says, "Hey, wait, is that goal **Realistic or Attainable?**", which **suggests** you should **limit yourself** and set a lesser or **smaller goal. No one should limit or change your goals**, and a goal-setting method that inherently does that is not the best method.

If Christopher Columbus, Madame Curie, Thomas Edison, the Wright Brothers, Henry Ford, Steve Jobs, Oprah, Jeff Bezos, or Elon Musk had bothered to follow a method insisting on "Realistic" and "Achievable" goals, our World would be a significantly less advanced and less wonderful place. There is nothing wrong with hard, or outrageous, or impossible goals.

A **change** was **needed**, so I took the most **effective** and **proven techniques** and practices from various goal-setting and goal-achievement processes and **created** a **new process**, a new **system** for success, **the D.R.E.A.M. Method.**

Benefits of the D.R.E.A.M. Method

A method is a systematic process that is a series of actions or steps usually performed in a specific order to achieve a particular result. People typically design processes and systems to maximize efficiency and effectiveness, and minimize confusion, and that's what the **D.R.E.A.M. Method does**. Following a method or process like the **D.R.E.A.M. Method** makes goal achievement easier.

There is **only one D.R.E.A.M. Method:** the one presented in this book, so you can follow the **same system/process every time.**

The benefits of the **D.R.E.A.M. Goal-Setting and Goal-Achievement Method** are:

- It's a **step-by-step process** that is the same every time.

- It's **easy-to-follow** structure that **helps you focus** on planning and execution of your actions, thereby increasing your chance of success in reaching your goals.

- Its **flexibility** allows use for any type of goal—personal, business, individual, or group, and allows for easily made adjustments to your **Action Plans**.

- It helps you with **accountability by Monitoring** your progress. By measuring the results of your actions, you can see your progress and **make** any necessary **adjustments** to keep you on track toward your goal.

- It **encourages you** to celebrate your successes and reward yourself because positive reinforcement will lead to more positive behavior and YOUR GOAL ACHIEVEMENT and SUCCESS!

For a Group

You can also use the **D.R.E.A.M. Method** for group goals as long as the overall goal for the group is the same. For example, a sales team typically has the same overall goal like a certain amount of sales. For group goals, I would go through the **D.R.E.A.M.** process together to help ensure everyone gets the same information and understands the overall goal and each individual's responsibilities. Then, in the Action Plan step, you would typically assign distinct steps/activities to specific individuals or smaller groups. To monitor progress, after the individuals or smaller groups report their results, managers or the entire group can decide on any adjustments.

Author's Note: If you are using the SMART method or any other method successfully, then I say keep going. However, I still recommend learning the **D.R.E.A.M.** Method, and hopefully, you find something you can use that helps you be even more successful.

Now that the overall framework of the **D.R.E.A.M.** method is explained, we will go through and learn the five individual steps of the system.

> *You don't rise to the level of your goals.*
> *You fall to the level of your system.*
>
> – James Clear

CHAPTER 5

Decide: What You Want, in Detail, by When

… the people who are crazy enough to think they can change the world are the ones who do.

– Attributed to Steve Jobs

THE BULLDOG

Ruben was originally from Argentina and moved to America when he was 12 years old. In his book, *The Courage to Succeed*, Ruben Gonzalez explains that, like many kids, he always dreamed of being an Olympian. He watched the 1980 Winter Olympics and the US Hockey Team's "Miracle on Ice" win over the Russians, which inspired him. And in 1984, after watching US underdog figure skater Scott Hamilton win a gold medal, **Ruden decided he was going to compete in the next Olympics.**

At the time, Ruben was 21 years old, an average athlete, and a benchwarmer on his college soccer team in Houston, Texas, so he knew he would not be playing soccer in the Olympics. But he was serious about his goal, so now he **had to decide on an event/ sport** to compete in.

He researched all the Olympic sports and chose the most physically demanding, the luge. If you don't know, the luge is a tiny sled you lie on and go downhill on a frozen track at over 80 miles per hour. And, oh yeah, you don't have any brakes. He **picked the luge** because many people gave up in that sport, and that played to **his strength,** which was his mental toughness. He was the "bulldog."

Ruben decided his goal was to compete in the luge competition at the 1988 Winter Olympics.

Bam! That people is the first step.

STEP 1 OF THE D.R.E.A.M. GOAL-SETTING AND GOAL-ACHIEVEMENT METHOD IS TO DECIDE: WHAT YOU WANT, IN DETAIL, BY WHEN.

Decide

The **first step** is to **Decide** on a **goal. Decide** on **what you want,** something that you want **to be, to have, to do, or to achieve.** It can be anything, maybe it's something you've only dreamed about doing. That's okay. You can turn dreams into reality, but you must make that decision. Yes, deciding for some people is the most difficult step in the goal-setting process. That's okay.

Hopefully, the exercises in Chapters 1 and 2 got you thinking about your goals. later in this chapter, there are a few additional tips and hacks to help you clarify and decide on a goal.

Did you think about some of your dreams or goals? Do you want to be an Olympian too? What do you truly desire? What is your

ideal vision of your life? What do you want to achieve personally, professionally, and spiritually? Who do you want standing next to you or watching you reach your goals?

Everyone has dreams, desires, wants, intentions, or goals, and they can all mean the same thing. For example, I dream of owning, desire to own, want to own, intend to own, and have a goal of owning a Ferrari. So, what's the difference between them? Dreams, desires, intentions, and wants are more general in nature. For goal-setting and goal-planning purposes, it is generally accepted that **goals are more specific**. For example, a desire for more money or a new car is a worthy desire, but they are not a good goal. To transform them into goals, they need to be more specific and **more detailed**, like specifying a dollar amount or a particular make, model, and year of that car.

Describe in Detail

Good goals include all the details about what we want, so after you Decide what you want, you need to describe your goal in detail. Everyone's goals are slightly different, so all the details about your goal matter. The details of your goal are what make your goal and your journey unique, so describe, in detail, exactly what you want.

Another reason to describe your goal in detail is motivation. A **generally defined goal** will only **inspire** a **general level** of **motivation** and action. Having a detailed, **very specific goal** or definite purpose **instills more desire** and **motivation,** which leads to more action. Your definite purpose, which is your main or most important goal, is a goal that will motivate you to take action. The more detailed and specific you are, the better. It's the details that make your goal more personal and help build motivation.

Finally, to make your goal proper, you need to have a **specific date** or deadline by which **to achieve your goal**. Having a specific date or deadline forces us to take action if we are serious about that goal. Even if there are no real consequences for not meeting a deadline, people will still think and feel more about that goal if there is a deadline. It's like running late to something. People feel more anxiety when they are running late, even if it's just a few minutes, because there is an expectation of that deadline. Setting a **date and time** for your goal **creates an expectation** in you and motivates you to take action.

Another reason for an **end date** for reaching your goal is **Parkinson's Law**. Parkinson's Law is really **an observation of a phenomenon**, not a scientific law, that finds **work expands to fit the time available to complete a task**. Meaning, if people are given two weeks to complete a task, they typically finish in two weeks. However, if people are given a month to do the same task, they tend to take the full month to complete it rather than finish in two weeks.

Goal Examples

Here are some **examples** of how to write your goals out:

Bad goals: because they lack details.

1. To lose weight this summer- is not a good goal because it's not specific in weight or time.
2. Make more money- is not a good goal because it does not specify the amount of money you want, and there is no time frame.
3. Buy a new house next year-is not a good goal because there are no specifics about the house, and next year is not a specific date.

Great goals: because amounts, timeframes, and details are specific.

1. I will weigh 190 lbs. on September 1, 2026.
2. I will be making $10,000 a month by September 30, 2026.
3. By December 31, 2026, I will buy my dream house, which is a one-story, four-bedroom with a study, three bathroom, all brick house with an extra-large, jacuzzi bathtub in the main bathroom, covered patio with a built-in grill, and a hot tub.

Write Your Goals Down

To further help you accomplish your goals, you should **write your goals down**. Yes, I mean actually write your goals down **in your own handwriting**. This step is **super important** for several reasons. First, by writing your goals down, you are taking the **first step** of **bringing something** that is **non-physical (your goal), into** the **physical world.** You are taking your thoughts that only exist in your head and creating something that exists in the material world. Your thoughts turned into words on a piece of paper are now real. You can see, feel, and hear them if read aloud.

Second, **writing** your **goal** down **engages** more learning and memory responses in **your brain** that typing does not. While obviously you can't see your brain's response, it is something that is occurring in the physical world that started with the non-physical. You writing your goal and seeing it creates a stronger memory of it and a stronger emotional connection to it.

If you can't write, then dictate onto your phone or computer, or get someone to write it for you. What would **stand out** more, a plain piece of computer paper filled with all uniform letters and words, or seeing **your handwritten words** on that same piece of paper? I suggest getting a **notebook** or a large notepad for the sole purpose of **writing down all of your** goals, so you have your own **goal notebook**. If you already journal, you can use the same kind of notebook but have a separate one for your goals.

The Study

You want **more reasons** or **proof** that you should **write down your goals**? In 2015, Dominican University of California issued a press release on the findings of their Psychology Professor, Dr. Gail Matthews, who conducted a study on goal achievement. **The study** aimed to **explore** how goal achievement if **effected by writing goals** and the **impact of accountability and support** on goal achievement. The participants were assigned different actions to take concerning their goals.

The **study showed:**

- The **group** that **kept** their **goals to themselves**, without writing them down, had a **42% success rate.**

- The **group** that **wrote down their goals had a 60% success rate.**

- The group that **wrote down** their goals, **shared them** with a friend, and **sent weekly progress reports** to the friend, **had a 76% success rate** in achieving their goals.

Other studies have also found that those who received **additional support** in the form of **coaching** or support from a **mentor** had **success rates as high as 80%.** In addition, people with a **mentor from their field of interest** of their goal reported **success rates of 85% and above.**

***

*** SECRET ***

Simply by writing down your goal, you significantly improved your chances of achieving that goal.

***

If you've already written a goal down, congratulations! If you haven't written any goals down, what are you waiting for? You can **start right NOW!**

Developing Your Goals

Not sure about what specifically you want? It's understandable and is a common situation for many people. To help you, there are multiple methods or exercises that will help you write down your goals. The **best method**, suitable for all types of people, all ages, and situations, is just making a list. Simply get a **sheet of paper,** start **brainstorming,** and **write** down a list of all the goals, dreams, and desires you can think of. Write down all the things that you **want** to **be**, **have**, **do**, and **achieve**. Five to ten goals will be easy. 20 gets hard for most people. If you get to 100, that's awesome. Great job. Yes, I'm serious-100. **Do not set limits**.

You can go to **icandream.net** under **Resources** and download the Goal List forms or use the ones in the Appendices section in the back of this book.

Goal Discovery Techniques/Prompts:

- **List** all the goals you can think of.

- **Describe your ideal day** and write it out**.** What does your ideal day look like? Where are you when you wake up, in a house, condo, etc.? Do you work out, cook breakfast, or go to work? What is your occupation? How do you get to work? Is there someone living with you? What do you do for fun? Then describe your ideal **week, month**, and **year**.

- **Describe** your **ideal income** or **amount of money** you want, and what it provides you with or allows you to do?

- **Year milestones**: In 1, 5, 10, and 15 years, write out all the things you want to have **accomplished or to be doing** at that time.

When writing your goals, make sure to **describe** them in as **much detail as possible**. Goals that you can describe in great detail tend to be the ones that are more important to you, even if you didn't think they were that important to you. Also, don't forget to include any people with whom you would like to achieve some of these goals, or at least share your success.

Another technique is what I call a **reflective** list. Spend a few hours or a day thinking about all the things that **you want to be**, to **have**, to **do**, and to **achieve**. Then, at the **end of the day**, **write down** the things/**goals** that **you remember** or that come to mind. This method should provide you with a list of goals that are the most important to you, as they are the ones you've had time to think about and that you remember.

Again, **keep a goal notebook** or journal with **all your goals** written down and **review your goals** regularly, **daily** if they are ones you are currently working on. When reviewing your goals, you will probably notice that **some goals feel more important** than others. That is good. There are reasons things jump out at you. Trust your intuition. **Reflect** on those goals and **develop** them further by describing them in more detail. If you review a goal and think or feel it's no longer important to you, then cross it out and move on.

No Career, No Problem

One area where I see many high school and college-age people struggle with is deciding on a career. It is a big decision and one that should not be made lightly. As a result, that decision is often avoided or delayed. My friend Mike changed his major in college so many times and took so many undergraduate courses that even the university finally told him to pick a major.

If you are in a similar situation, in addition to making an **Experience List,** I suggest taking an **online career and/or interest assessment**. There are multiple websites where you can find these types of assessments, which are also called tests, inventories, and profilers. Complete a few and go over the results with an adult who knows you well and see if they agree. Then, follow your intuition and pick one. Remember, you can always change your mind and do something else.

You can find links to a few of these websites at **icandream.net** under Resources.

Your Uniqueness Matters

Your age, experience, and situation do matter, and those factors will influence the type of goals you have. For example, an older or more established person may already have some of the material things that a younger person may desire. **Remember,** they are **your goals**, and it's **your journey**, not anyone else's.

Most people can usually write a few big goals or dreams down quickly but then struggle with the finer details or specifics about their goals. If you aren't struggling, then that's great. If you are, no worries, just keep at it. **Thinking about specific details will help you discover what you truly want**. If you can't imagine details about a specific goal, then maybe it's not as important as you first thought. It's okay to change your mind.

Also, remember, there are no limits, so write down every goal you think of as that starts the goal achievement process. And if you still **haven't started**, then **stop reading**, get your **goal notebook** out, and **start writing** your goals down right **now**, and **make them real!** Writing your goals down is believing in them, and that's the first step to achieving those goals and **how you** begin **transform-ing** your life from ordinary to extraordinary!

Narrowing Your Goals

When you think your goal list is complete, then **number your top five goals in order of importance**. This part can be harder, but you need to narrow down what is most important to you, at least for right now. You may find that some of the goals you thought of first are not as important as you first thought. And that's okay, don't worry, because there are no wrong answers. Often, when we think more about something, we change our minds about it. The idea is to narrow down to an important goal that you can start working on immediately.

Goal Time Frames

When looking at your goal list, you should observe that **your goals** have **different time frames**. Your goal to lose weight is something you probably want to start working on right away. While your goal to have children may be five to ten years away, and a goal to retire at age 50 could be ten or more years away.

The length of goal time frames varies from resource to resource, but most are similar. I am designating the **goal time frame cate-gories** as short-term, medium/mid-term, and long-term. The length of time for those **goal time frame categories** are as follows:

Short-term: 0 to 12 months
Medium-term: 1 to 2 years
Long-term: 2 years or longer

And I add **another category** of **lifetime goals**. These are specific goals that most people want to achieve on an **ongoing basis**, like eating healthy, exercising, being mindful, and practicing spirituality.

The **ideal plan** is for you to turn as many of your **lifetime goals** into habits as possible. How? **By setting them as goals**, and then taking **persistent actions** toward achieving them. **One step, one action, one day at a time**.

Studies show that it takes **20 to 90 days** to form a **new habit or** to **break** an **old one**. Also, the **greatest influencers** on the **length of time** it takes to **form a habit** are **frequency**, how often you repeat the behavior, **and** the **level of emotion** attached to the behavior. Again, it's why choosing goals that inspire you is so important.

*** SECRET ***

The more often you take action on a goal and the more important that goal is to you, the faster you can turn that goal into a habit.

Your First Goal

The **best way to start** goal-setting and goal-achievement is to **choose** a **short-term goal** to work on first. By working on a short-term goal first, you can **develop your skills** with the goal-setting and goal-achievement process. More importantly, you can **experience** the **joy** and **sense of accomplishment** in achieving one of your goals sooner rather than later. Hopefully, you will use the momentum of your success to continue your goal-setting and goal-achievement and reach for even bigger goals.

While it is important to challenge oneself and strive for improvement, it is probably best to start with a goal that you know is achievable for the reasons given above. Setting a really difficult goal at first can lead to frustration and disappointment if you are unable to achieve it. However, if you have a really challenging goal, and you're determined to achieve it, and it's your burning desire, then, by all means, start working on it.

Also, I recommend **starting with a Health goal** for several reasons. First, most health goals, like losing weight, fall into the short-term category even if they are also lifetime goals. Also, **improving your Health will help you achieve other goals**. When you get proper sleep, you function better both mentally and physically. The same is true with eating healthy and exercising, so consider starting with a Health goal.

*** SECRET ***

Your Health is the most important goal category as its benefits give you the biggest help overall and is a catalyst for success with your other goals.

Goal Categories

There are many areas or categories that goals fall into, like financial goals or health goals. It's important to be aware of them, especially when doing advanced planning, because most goals will affect other areas or goals in your life. The most relevant example is your Health.

When you have really poor health, it affects all areas of your life. Then it usually becomes the most important goal, and often the only one you can focus on.

Different sources have different goal categories. However, regardless of the source, most have five to eight similar goal categories that they use to classify goals. I believe these six categories cover most goals.

The Goal Categories are: Health, Career, Financial, Social, Spirituality, and Personal Growth.

Health: Nutrition, Exercise, Sleep, Relaxation, Hygiene

This category covers your **physical, mental, and emotional health and well-being.** I included five subcategories to help educate people on the different areas included in health. I don't think Nutrition, Exercise, and Sleep need further explanation. Relaxation includes what you do for fun, or to release stress, like watching TV, playing video games, hobbies, or just time for your mind and body to recover. There are some activities, like walking, that can be both Exercise and Relaxation. Hygiene is not just taking a bath or shower and brushing your teeth. It's also keeping your clothes and your environment clean, especially your home. Good hygiene helps prevent diseases and other conditions and promotes health, yet we sometimes take it for granted and overlook its importance.

When you are healthy, you function better mentally and physically and can handle more emotional stress. You can do physical work longer, focus on tasks longer, and maintain motivation or discipline for longer periods of time. Also, when people are healthy, they have more confidence in themselves. All of these factors lead to more success in achieving your other goals as well, which is why **your Health is**, or should be, your **most important goal category**.

Career(s)/Occupation(s)

This category covers **your job, what you do for a living,** or **how you make money**. The "s" is there because in today's world, most people will have more than one career or occupation during their lifetime. Also, these days, a side hustle is the norm rather than the exception. It also includes your goals within your job, like getting into management, and other professional achievements you want to achieve, like becoming a Certified Public Accountant (CPA).

For parents, yes: a full-time parent or unpaid caretaker is arguably the most important job. Even though you don't receive direct payment for this type of work, you should still include it in your long-term planning. These types of jobs are a good example for planning on multiple occupations, as these jobs typically have a natural cycle and an end date. As a parent, you may one day hear your child tell you to stop parenting them. And it may be true. Then, it is time for another job.

The amount of money you make from your job/occupation directly relates to your Financial/Lifestyle goals, and also Social goals.

Financial/Lifestyle

This category covers a wide range of areas and goals and includes **how you live and what you spend money on**. Areas in this category include where you live, what you live in, the type of car you drive, how you get from one place to another, what leisure activities you do, travel/vacation, your plans for retirement, and more.

This category will consume most of your time and money throughout your life. Therefore, the more goals you plan and achieve within it, the more effectively you will use your resources. You want to save time and money, right? Then it would be smart to start goal-setting and goal-achievement.

Social: Friends, Family, Significant Other, Work, and Other Groups

This category covers your **relationships with other people**. I think it **affects people's** lives **more than** they **realize** because the people in our lives do influence our thoughts and behaviors. Most people have a few lifelong relationships with a family member or friend, or long friendships at work. I have several friends that I've known for over 45 years and people at my job for over 30 years. Think about if you had a terrible falling out with a person who you've known most of your life, or your significant other, wouldn't that affect you? Wouldn't you be upset or disappointed? Of course you would. And the effect could last a long time; hence, the importance of relationships, taking care of them, and considering them when planning.

As we go through life, our **Social circles change**. You will have multiple relationships at **schools**, in your **neighborhoods**, **workplaces**, and even with multiple **families.** Many of you are already planning Social goals, you just didn't realize it.

If you are married or have a significant other, what happens when the holidays come around? Most couples discuss, or argue, about whose house/family they are going to and how much time they will spend there. Just an FYI, it helps if you plan those things out and compromise. If you have children, or are planning on having children, you are definitely a Social planner and will be for a long time.

Many people join groups for hobbies, or to network, or for a vast variety of reasons, which are examples of Social goal planning and achievement. Please keep up the good work.

Finally, most people know, or have an idea, what they want their significant other to be like. It is good to know what you want, especially when it comes to the person you will spend most of your time with. While most relationships occur organically because of the circumstances, like school or work, others require planning and effort on your part. Since you will have various types of relationships, include your

Social goals when doing long-term planning to make the best of them.

Spirituality/Religion

This category covers your spiritual and religious beliefs and practices. There are many definitions for **Spirituality**, so I'm referring to it as your **beliefs** and **feelings about being part of a greater world and universe** than yourself, while **Religion** is more of a **set of beliefs and practices** concerning a God or higher power.

For many people, their spirituality or religion is something they experience as a journey over their lifetimes as they gain experience and knowledge. It is part of being a better person or a better version of yourself. These goals are often part of people's Personal Growth goals, like wanting to learn more about their religion or to volunteer more at their place of worship. Spirituality and religion are a big part of most societies and can have a tremendous influence on our lives, so don't overlook these types of goals when planning

Personal Growth

This area encompasses all **Personal Development** and Self-actualization. Personal Growth is **realizing** and **expressing one's full potential** in your various interests, like creativity, knowledge, and genuine happiness. Examples include learning another language, doing more volunteer work, learning how to cook more things, or teaching others.

These goals are ones that make you a better, happier, or more fulfilled person. Often, these goals start off with people saying, "I've always wanted to do ______," or "I've always wanted to go to ______." Many of these goals are what people plan to do when they retire. These goals often represent delayed gratification. We have wanted to travel, but we have been busy working, raising kids, or taking care of elderly parents, or all of the above. Hopefully, you can achieve some of these wants and goals.

What Goal Categories Should You Plan For?

Ideally, you should make goals in **all** the **categories**. You decide, but you should be aware of all the facts. For example, studies have shown that people who achieve all their external or physical goals, i.e.. the house they want, the car they want, and still end up feeling empty inside. While people who achieved internal goals, like helping others, reported higher levels of happiness.

However, there are **no wrong answers**. I say that to encourage you and so that you **do not limit yourself**. You don't have to pick just one career or job. It's okay to change goals and do something else you like more. If you want to **do different things**, then do them, **but plan them** out, so you **don't waste** your **time or other resources.**

In Chapter 11, in the **Advanced Goal Planning** section, you will find more detailed information on long-term planning.

If you want to be a happy man, you should tie your life to a goal, not to other people and not to things.

– Albert Einstein

CHAPTER 6

Resources:
Ones You Have and Ones You Need

Success is a team sport.

– Simon Sinek

*Remember, no one can make it alone. Have no
shame in asking for help when you need it.*

– Sandra Day O'Connor

OFF TO LAKE PLACID

After Ruben Gonzalez decided on his goal to luge in the next Olympics, he had to move to Lake Placid, New York, to learn how to luge and train at the US Olympic training facility. He didn't have any sponsors giving him money, so he had to pay for all his expenses himself. First, he used all of his own money. Next, he used all his credit on his credit cards. Then, he had to borrow money from family and friends.

Ruben had to learn to luge, and learning at his age was very hard, both mentally and physically. He needed a coach. Do you think the fact that Ruben's coach was a previous World Champion luge winner helped Ruben? Of course it did. Besides financial help, Ruben's **friends** and **family** also provided the **emotional support** he needed. Even on day one, Ruben needed some emotional support, which he received from a family friend who was wise enough to know Ruben would need it.

STEP 2 OF THE D.R.E.A.M. GOAL-SETTING AND GOAL-ACHIEVEMENT METHOD IS RESOURCES: ONES YOU HAVE AND ONES YOU NEED.

Resources

Resources are the **things you have or need that help you accomplish your goals**. Resources can be **physical** things like money, equipment, property, or people with certain skills. They can also be **non-physical** things like your credit score, a company's goodwill, insurance, a patent, or specific skills, like accounting or writing skills, that you need to acquire in order to achieve your goal.

In conversations with people about their goals and **Resources**, I found that people do not spend much time thinking about all the resources available to them. They viewed Resources in a casual way, and more as part of their Action Plan. They did not see them as a separate planning step or being that important.

Hopefully, after reading this chapter, you will see the importance of Resources in planning for your goals and their power in helping you accomplish your goals.

Your Resources

After you decide on your goal, you need to make a list of the **Resources You Have and Ones You Need.** The best way to discover your resources is to simply brainstorm. **Brainstorming** is both a **creative process** that can be used to generate new ideas and a **problem-solving technique** that can help you generate a variety of options. When you brainstorm, do not filter your thoughts and **write down anything** and **everything that comes to mind** when thinking about your topic.

When brainstorming your Resources, ask yourself: What resources do you currently have to help you accomplish your goal? **Write** down the **Resources You Have** in one **column**. Then, think about and write down the **Resources You Need** in another **column**. Brainstorming about resources can often help you realize that you have more resources than you initially thought, and/or it can help you realize needed or helpful resources that you hadn't thought about before.

Other benefits of brainstorming are that it increases creativity and helps people think outside the box. While **this step**/process may not initially seem important, it **is very important. Brainstorming** the right way can help you **break free** of your **usual thought patterns** and **limiting beliefs**, and generate a wider range of options, alternative solutions, and new ideas.

You are Your Best Resource

When thinking about and looking for resources, start by looking at yourself and then work your way out. First, **what resources do You personally bring** to the starting line of your goal-achievement process? Money? Credit? List your personal physical and non-physical resources you have to achieve your goal.

Next, in the process of working your way out, are your friends and family. What resources do your friends and family have that are available to you? If you are working on a business/occupational goal, then look for resources there. Coworkers, managers, company benefits, and even competitors can be possible resources for you.

For a younger person, think of someone who you believe has knowledge about your goal, or someone you trust to guide you to appropriate resources, and then ask that person what they know about your goal. Chances are, you will gain some knowledge or at least get information on another possible resource.

Don't Let Pride Stop You

Many people don't like the thought of asking friends, family, or anyone for help. Asking for help makes them uncomfortable, and they don't want to appear incapable. I get it. However, this concern is usually an unjustified fear, and in short, it's something you need to move past. If you can't bring yourself to ask for help from anyone so that you can accomplish your dreams/goals, then I say that goal must not be that important to you. Because **if** it is **truly important** to you, you will put aside your pride or ego and **ask for help**. You should want and **accept help so you can reach your goal faster**.

Also, people's readiness and willingness to help may surprise you. People often want to help others, but they don't want to offend the other person or appear too forward by asking the other person if they need help. Helping others is a form of giving that people get personal satisfaction from doing, so they will jump at the chance to help you if you just ask. And people like to be asked.

Toward the end of one luge season, right before the Olympics, Ruben Gonzalez had a terrible crash, which broke several bones and completely destroyed his sled. Ruben didn't have enough money to buy another sled, but there was no way he was going to give up on his goal. He asked a competitor and ended up **borrowing** that **competitor's extra sled** to qualify for and race in the 2002 Winter Olympics. His competitor was happy to help, so **never overlook or undervalue** the possible **help** available from other people. Their help might be what helps you accomplish your goal or dream. **Resources Example:**

Example of Ruben's Resources:

<u>**Ones He Had:**</u>	<u>**Ones He Needed:**</u>
training facility	equipment
some money	financial support
some credit	coach
support of friends/family	emotional support
	medical support

Resources for my weight loss **goal to weigh 190 pounds** are as follows:

<u>**Have:**</u>	<u>**Need:**</u>
The internet, diet, and exercise books,	Specific exercise plan(s)
Row machine, bicycle, big exercise ball,	Diet plan
25 lbs. dumbbells, floor space,	Accountability Partner
Pair of tennis shoes	

Troy, my friend who was a triathlon competitor, to help me create exercise and diet plans. Also, I can use him as an accountability partner.

Another example: Let's say you have a goal of opening a franchise business, and you need $100,000 for the franchise startup costs/ fee. For **Resources**, you

Have:	**Need:**
$50,000 in cash	$50,000 (cash or loan)
Small piece of property worth $25,000	
Excellent credit score	

So, with your good credit score and a piece of property as collateral, you can get a business loan for the other $50k. Other options could be to sell the property, then get an unsecured loan for $25k, or rent the property and save that income, and get a smaller loan. By **brainstorming** and **listing** all of your **resources**, you are **better able to see and think of possible solutions** to achieving your goal. Also, after seeing all of your resources, you may realize that you are closer to achieving your goal than you thought.

For Group Resources

If you are using the **D.R.E.A.M. Method** for a group project, then you would list all the people in your group as Resources You Have. Then, you can ask each person what skills they have or have access to that pertain to your common goal, and have them write out the Resources they bring to the project. This step would also serve as a good team-building exercise.

The Resource Cheat Code

In today's World, we have the **best research tool** available, which is also the **Resource Cheat Code,** and that, of course, **is the Internet**. I didn't start this chapter with the Resource Cheat Code because I want people to learn/develop their critical thinking and problem-solving skills, and the brainstorming part of this step helps develop those skills. Also, following the process helps build emotional ties to your goal, which improves your motivation and action.

Besides, the Resource Cheat Code is the next thing you should do after brainstorming. "Wait, Ron, are you saying we should use the Cheat Code?" Yes, I am! Cheat away.

Doing **research on your goal and educating yourself** about it by reviewing all the information you can find **is an invaluable step**. You can search for pretty much anything. Just minutes of research can lead to discovering new and/or important information about your goal, save you hours of effort or other resources, and help you reach your goal faster. In most situations, it is an essential tool for researching and planning for your goal.

In Chapter 2, I said, "You can't copy someone else's homework," because your goals and your journey are unique to you. With that said, you don't need to reinvent the wheel either. Meaning, there are **proven actions, processes, steps, and resources** available that can help you achieve your goals. And there is nothing wrong with modeling actions/steps that work. That is called **working smarter**, not harder.

To better prepare yourself for a goal, especially one that is more difficult, **do an internet search on "resources required/needed to (state your specific goal.)"** For example, in your favorite search engine, type **"Resources for losing weight."** When I did this search, it showed there were over 130 million results. I'm pretty sure that you can find all the information you need about resources available to you for most any goal. Also, I suggest you **look at several pages** of responses, to see a wider variety, which may reveal a less common resource that could be exactly what you need. Then, try the same **search in two or more** different **search engines**, again, just so you see a wider variety of responses.

Look for resources that are **not on your lists** and decide if you need them or not. Most people will be surprised by the number of resources already available for all kinds of goals. Also, **look for**

proven resource lists and use them.

Here are a few examples of resource prompts you can use:

- **How to** (your goal). For example, how to lose weight
- **The best way to** (lose weight) and you can add more **specific descriptions**, for example, (. . . for people/men/women over 50)
- **Resources for** (losing weight)
- **Free resources for** (your goal)

After you do your research, you may end up with a giant list of resources. That is a good thing. Next, just go through them and decide which ones you need and which are the best for you.

Artificial Intelligence

AI is here to stay, and the younger you are the more AI will be a part of your life. My **suggestion** to everyone, especially younger generations, is to **take an AI course as soon as possible** and incorporate it into your life as much as possible.

With AI, you can be even more specific and creative in your searches. You can create prompts or questions for AI that are tailored to your exact situation. You can tell AI what resources you have and ask it what other resources you need for your specific goal. The more detailed your prompt is the more detailed its response should be. Also, you are not limited in using it just for Resources. You can use it for any type of search or situation. My only suggestion is that you use more than one source so you can gain additional results and **verify information**. It's a great tool that can help you, and you should learn how to use it.

Choosing the Best Resources

Many factors go into choosing the best resources, including which ones you **need**, their **availability**, their **costs**, and which ones are the **best for you** and your situation. For both physical and non-physical resources, there are usually all kinds of **product reviews** that you can find online that can help you narrow down choices.

Each type of resource has its own advantages and disadvantages, which you should consider before committing to one. Again, **researching** resources and **educating yourself** will help you **choose the best** resources to aid you in achieving your goal.

Your Learning Style

If you need an educational or informational resource, your preferred learning style—visual, auditory, read/write, or kinesthetic/tactile—will probably affect which resources you choose. However, when you are trying to accomplish a goal, I suggest choosing the **most effective method for you**. For example, you may like reading the most, but if you learn and remember more by watching a video, then you should watch videos. Yes, your preference should be considered, but your **goal achievement is the priority** here. Right? You can always read something during your relaxation time. Also, you are **not limited to just one learning style**, so you can select your preferred style, the most effective one, or all of them.

Common Resources: the internet, books, audiobooks, apps, blogs, videos, podcasts, webinars, courses, coaches, mentors, teachers, and friends.

- **The internet**: You can search the internet for "how to" do anything and pretty much find something every time, or research and get information on any topic.

- **Books, blogs, and printed materials**: can provide a large amount of information and very detailed information. However, they don't provide interaction or feedback and tend to take more time.

- **Videos, webinars (recorded), audiobooks, and podcasts:** are very convenient and can benefit both visual and auditory learners, and there are literally thousands or millions of videos on every subject. Their downside can be that their quality, accuracy, and relevance to your goal may be limited.

- **Live webinars:** can provide you with the same convenience of videos, add more interaction, and personalized information. However, their dates and times of availability can be limited or not at convenient times for you.

- **Apps:** can help you track your progress toward your goals and provide you with a variety of options. However, they may not be compatible or customizable to meet your goals.

- **Courses (online or In-person):** can provide you with structured, interactive, and comprehensive learning, but they may be expensive and/or time-consuming.

The Secret Resources are...

The Secret Resources are **Coaches, Mentors, Teachers, Friends, and Accountability Partners**. They can provide personalized guidance, first-hand knowledge, expertise, feedback, and support. Their downside is that some of them, who are professionals, may be expensive or have limited availability for time or location. However, their benefits clearly outweigh any downsides.

*** SECRET ***

In terms of increasing your odds of achieving your goal, after simply writing down your goal, <u>having a coach or mentor provides the biggest increase in your chance of achieving your goal.</u>

Often included in lists of **characteristics of successful people** are **teamwork** and **collaboration.** These characteristics demonstrate the value and **importance** of people **working together.** In Steven Covey's ***The 7 Habits of Highly Effective People,*** **Habit 6, Synergize: Principles of Creative Cooperation,** emphasizes the power of people working together.

In Jack Canfield's ***The Success Principles***, Part III is titled "Build Your Success Team," and he has 9 Success Principles dedicated to this section. Of note are "**Principle 41, Build a Powerful Support Team and Delegate to Them,**" and "**Principle 45, Hire a Personal Coach.**"

Because of its importance, I'm going to state that point again, another way; **Jack Canfield,** one of the most successful success coaches, **advises that you should hire a personal coach.** So please understand the **importance of these Resources.** After using a coach or mentor, I'm certain you will see their benefit and power. Adding a **coach** or **mentor** to your list of **needed Resources** is always a smart move.

The Power of Support

Other valuable resources are **accountability partners, support persons,** or a **support team**. Just being **accountable** to someone helps increase your chances of goal achievement. While having a coach or mentor there to advise or teach you on specific skills or actions to take, a support team or person can **help you stay motivated** when you are having difficulties. After Ruben Gonzalez's first day of training, he felt like quitting and called a family friend who helped him get through that momentary lapse of self-belief. Support teams or persons are there **for emotional support**. That's it.

Are you thinking, "Ron, do you really want me to **get a cheerleader?" Heck yes**, I do. You can call the person whatever you want: a cheerleader, a motivation coach, a support person, or your mental fortitude instructor, but **they work!** Think back, do you remember a time when someone, a coach, a teacher, a friend, or a family member ever said to you, "You can do it." How **powerful** was that support? Didn't it make you feel better and give you some motivation?

If you can't remember someone saying that to you or no one ever has, then, **I'm telling you** right now, **You CAN do it!** Whatever your goal is, just **follow the D.R.E.A.M. process**, and **you can and will succeed.**

Having people support you is a big help. Look at college and professional football. The **team's supporters**, i.e., their fans, in their home stadiums have become **known as the 12ᵗʰ Man.** Why do you think most sports teams have a better record when playing at their home stadium or gym? Hundreds or thousands of **people cheering** for and **supporting you** is a **powerful thing, and** so is **just one** person who is there specifically for **you.**

People's motivation typically only lasts for so long, especially when obstacles arise. You may need a pep talk or just a little encouragement to help you keep going. And if your Support Team or Person

helps you to keep going when you feel like quitting, and you **reach your goal, how valuable would their help be?**

One of my **Support Persons** was a coworker and is a friend who has always been appreciative and supportive of me. Her personal and professional advice and continued encouragement of me to finish this book was very helpful and inspirational. She has been my example of self-belief and perseverance for years. You will meet her in Chapter 10, the **Best in the World.**

Who is your **cheerleader**? Don't know? Well, **add** that to your list of **Resources: You Need.**

In Summary

Resources are very important in helping you accomplish your goals and, therefore, an important step in the goal-setting and goal-achievement process. Hopefully, during brainstorming, you can think of new ways or new resources to help in reaching your goals. Also, discovering that you need certain resources can help you in deciding the order in which you should do things.

While focusing on **Resources** may seem like a new concept, it's not. It's really about **better planning** and finding **support** to aid you in your goal achievement. This step and the next, **Evaluate,** will help you prepare for making your Action Plan.

Coach knows the shortcut to success.

– Ruben Gonzalez, Four-Time Olympian

CHAPTER 7

Evaluate:
Your Starting Situation
and the Best Route

As you head toward your goals, be prepared to make some slight adjustments to your course. You don't change your decision to go, you do change your direction to get there.

– Zig Ziglar

STEP 3 OF THE D.R.E.A.M. GOAL-SETTING AND GOAL-ACHIEVEMENT METHOD IS EVALUATE: YOUR STARTING SITUATION AND THE BEST ROUTE

Your Starting Situation

In **planning for How** to reach your goals, you need to know more than just your starting location. You need to **know your starting**

situation, so you can **determine the best route** to reach your goals. **Your Starting Situation** is a **combination** of your **goal**, your **resources**, and your **circumstances**. Your circumstances are all relevant **facts** and **conditions** that affect, or may affect, you in achieving your goal. These factors can include your current location, timeframe, time available, health, income, debt, needed equipment, needed skills, and any **current or potential obstacles**.

Current and Potential Obstacles

Experience teaches you that obstacles are part of life and that you should **expect them**. Are there any current obstacles affecting your goal achievement? If yes, what are they? What obstacles do you foresee running into? Again, using the driving example, you may find out that there is a road closure on the route you planned on taking. So now you need to **update your plan** by **Evaluating** the new circumstances and **choose** a different **Best Route**.

You should start thinking about existing and potential obstacles and how to best address them. Write those concerns down and ways to address them. This activity can provide you with a list of potential tasks for overcoming those obstacles to add into your **Action Plan** in the next step. It can also help you realize, or strengthen your self-belief, that you can achieve your goal as you find ways to address and overcome your obstacles. Obstacles are a very important issue and require a whole chapter (Chapter 10) to address them.

Your Best Route

Based on all the information about **your goal, resources,** and **circumstances,** you **chose** the **Best Route** to reach **your goal.** Your Best Route may or may not be the fastest, shortest, safest, or most common. Your Best Route is influenced by your unique experiences, circumstances, and goals.. Now, that does not mean you shouldn't use proven methods, techniques, or routes. It just means you should base your decisions on you, and not on what path someone else used.

For example, let's say you decided to achieve your **goal of driving across the United States**. You have a car and some money, and off you go. You pull out of your driveway, you get to the street corner near your home, and now, **which way should you go**? There are a number of highways you can take to drive across the US. Where are you going to stop for gas? Where are you going to spend the night? Do you have enough money to stay at hotels or are you going to sleep in your car? How much money did you plan to spend on food? And you probably want to complete this goal in a shorter time frame rather than a long one, right? Are there any current obstacles or known future obstacles, like road closures?

In the example above, knowing your starting location is easy. However, your **starting situation** is much more involved and consists of **many factors and information. Knowing** your starting situation will **help you make better decisions** in your planning. Usually, there are multiple ways or routes to reach your goal, so you do need to know all of those factors as they will help you to evaluate the **Best Route** to reach your goal.

Texas, New York, and Argentina

When Ruben Gonzalez called the US Olympic Training Facility in New York to find out where he needed to go to learn how to luge, the man on the phone told Ruben he was too old. Of course, that was not going to stop Ruben. While Ruben was explaining his situation to the man, Ruben mentioned he lived in Texas, but he was born in Argentina.

Then the man's attitude changed, and he explained that Ruben could represent Argentina in the Olympics, which would help keep the luge event in the Olympics. This news made Ruben even more excited. However, the man left out some pretty important information, like Argentina didn't have a luge team at the time, which was another step that Ruben had to take as part of his goal.

Ruben's starting situation for his goal of competing in the luge in the 1988 Olympics looked like this:

- Ruben was living in Texas but needed to **move to New York**

- He would have to **pay** for his **living expenses** and **equipment**

- He needed to **learn how to luge**

- And he would have to **convince** the country of **Argentina** that they needed **to have** a national **luge team**.

- And regardless of Argentina having a luge team, Ruben still **needed to be ranked** in the **top 50 in the World** to **qualify for the Olympics**.

- And all this had to be done in slightly **less than four years**.

Ruben's Best Route

Remember, it's **your situation**, your **goal**, and your **plan**, so **don't copy someone else's homework**. Ruben Gonzalez was the perfect example. He couldn't copy anyone because no one had been in his same situation. Based on Ruben's goal and starting situation, he only had a few routes to choose from. The most important and **highest priority** activity for him was to **learn how to luge**. If he couldn't learn to luge, then no other step or activity that he needed to complete would matter. Ruben's Best Route was to move to New York, learn to luge as fast as possible and start gaining experience, since he was starting from zero.

If you are thinking that it looks like Ruben had a very difficult starting situation and route, you are right; he did. It was very difficult and truly unique, but he succeeded because he kept working toward his goal, which proves you can too.

The Best Route to an Action Plan

Ideally, you want to choose the Best Route, which is the route that **gets you to your goal** in the **shortest time** while making the **best use of** your **resources**. The **Route** to your goal is really a **set of steps or actions** you must perform to **reach your goal**. So, for **Step 3 Evaluate**, you take all this information into consideration, then create your **Action Plan (Step 4, next chapter)** that best fits you and helps you achieve your goal.

Example of Starting Situation and Best Route:

For my **Goal** to **weigh 190 pounds on September 1, 2025,** my **Resources** to consider were as follows:

<u>Have:</u>	<u>Need:</u>
The Internet, diet and exercise books,	Specific exercise plan(s)
Row machine, bicycle, big exercise ball,	Diet plan
25 lbs. dumbbells, floor space,	Accountability Partner
Pair of tennis shoes	

Troy, my friend who was a triathlon competitor, to help me create exercise and diet plans. Also, I can use him as an accountability partner.

My **Starting Situation** was I weighed 213 lbs. and, based on my schedule, my free times were in the late afternoons. Also, my bad knees prohibited me from running or doing other high-impact exercises.

My **Best Route** was to plan on exercising 30 to 60 minutes in the afternoons. Meal prep on Sunday. I will do internet research and come up with weekly meal plans that fit me and get a specific weight-training plan from my fitness coach. Due to my bad knees, I will include alternate workouts of rowing, biking, and walking. Note: If I had access to a pool, I would include swimming as that is a great all-around, low-impact exercise, but I have to work with what I have available.

Reality Check

After **Evaluating** all the relevant facts, knowing your **Starting Situation**, and choosing the **Best Route**, do you still think your **goal is achievable** in your **desired timeframe?** Also, can you realistically **get** the **resources you need?** The purpose of these questions is to simply **help you focus on** the **planning** portion of the goal-achievement process to ensure you are prepared for your journey. These questions are not in any way to dissuade you from a goal. I am not asking if your goal is realistic or achievable, because I know it is. These questions are just a double-check, like looking in your wallet or purse to make sure you did put that money or credit card back in it. If you have doubts, you may need to make adjustments, such as increasing your timeframe or changing your goal or route.

Also, this **Evaluation** gives you a mental and emotional temperature **check** on **how important your goal is** to you. In some situations, after careful consideration, you may realize that you don't want to put the needed effort or money into that goal at this time and that's okay. This temperature check is important because it's your **goals that cause a "burning desire"** in you that you will **more likely** and **more easily achieve**. If you don't have a very strong emotional attachment to a goal, you are less likely to achieve that goal. Your **honesty** with yourself can **prevent** you from **wasting** your **time, effort**, or other **resources** on a goal that you are not fully committed to. Again, trust your intuition.

If it's a difficult goal that makes you unsure about your success, then that is actually a good thing. It is the **extra thought and effort** you put **into planning** your goals that **helps you find solutions, grow**, and **become a better person**, which ultimately helps you **achieve** those **difficult goals**. If it's a goal that you know you will easily accomplish, then you may want to spend less time on any detailed planning.

If you decide your **goal** is **unrealistic** or **too difficult** for any reason, then you can simply **modify it**, like **extending** the **due date**, or break it down into **smaller steps/goals**. This **Evaluation** is part of choosing the Best Route. Sometimes big goals do need to be broken down into smaller ones. As you gain goal achievement experience, you will be able to better recognize when these situations occur.

In short, **Step 3: Evaluate**, is to **help discover the best way for You to succeed at reaching your goal** and help you **decide on needed actions/steps** that will go in your **Action Plan, Step 4**. Most importantly, the idea is to **not give up on your goal**, just modify it if needed. **Remember-You Can!**

Taking action will help you reach your goals. However, taking action without planning could cause you to waste time, money, or other resources.

Vision without action is a daydream.
Action without vision is a nightmare.

– Japanese Proverb

CHAPTER 8

Action Plan: Steps to Achieve Your Goal

The journey of a thousand miles starts with a single footstep.

– Lao Tzu

The above quote from Lao Tzu embodies goal achievement. You have a goal, and you have the activity that gets you to that goal. Even when facing a seemingly huge or difficult goal, you can still work towards it with a simple, single step. That's the **Action Plan**.

STEP 4 OF THE D.R.E.A.M. GOAL-SETTING AND GOAL-ACHIEVEMENT METHOD IS TO MAKE AN ACTION PLAN: STEPS TO ACHIEVE YOUR GOAL.

An **Action Plan** is a **list of specific steps/tasks/actions** that you need to complete to achieve your goal. It's **the How** of goal achievement. While your Action Plan can be as **simple** as a **list of steps**, it may need to be a **highly detailed**, daily, weekly, or monthly

schedule of tasks to be completed on specific days with specific times dedicated to those actions. The difficulty or complexity of the goal will usually indicate how detailed your Action Plan should be.

A good **example** of an **Action Plan** for a goal is **driving directions** to a specific place. For example, most people have seen or heard directions given from a roadway app. Those directions typically tell you how far to drive, what lane to be in, which way to turn, and when you have arrived at your destination. Action Plans **do not have to be complex. Simple is good**.

Ruben's Action Plan is Not Your Action Plan

Just like Ruben Gonzalez's starting situation, his **Action Plan** was very **unique to his situation** and his **goal.** His daily and weekly actions were very specific but common to his sport. However, the framework for an Action Plan of doing a specific activity, on a specific day, for a specific amount of time, is pretty simple and can apply to most goals.

A simple version for **Ruben's Action Plan** would look similar to the following:

Day/time	**Activity**
Monday:	Travel day, walk racetrack, take notes, eat healthy
Tuesday:	Review notes, watch/do practice runs, workout, eat healthy
Wednesday:	Practice runs, workout, eat healthy
Thursday:	Practice runs, workout, eat healthy
Friday:	Practice runs, workout, eat healthy
Saturday:	Competition day, eat healthy
Sunday:	Competition day, eat healthy

As you can see, an Action Plan does not have to be complicated, especially if you don't want it to be. If you already use a **weekly schedule or calendar** to keep track of your activities, then congratulations, you are already making an Action Plan. All you need to do now is keep track of your completed activities by putting a check mark next to, or circle around, the finished activity.

Why Make an Action Plan

Having an **Action Plan** to reach your goal is **like** having the **recipe** for your favorite dessert. A recipe tells you **what Resources** you need, then **what to do** with those resources, and **how long** you should do each step. Even if you have never made chocolate chip cookies before, if you simply **follow the recipe**, a.k.a. the **D.R.E.A.M. Method**, you can **enjoy** the yummy warm goodness that is **the result** of achieving your goal.

An Action Plan will **help you work** toward your goal in a **methodical** and **organized** manner. It tells you what to do and when to do it, which **maximizes** your **time management** and other **resources**. By making your plan and **establishing** the **priorities** and order of your actions, you help yourself **avoid decision fatigue** and allow yourself more time to **focus on** your **current task**. Finally, your Action Plan **establishes specific activity measurements** and a clear **timetable** that allows you to track your progress toward your goal.

How to Make an Action Plan

You should **arrange** your **list of actions**/steps in the **order** that best **maximizes efficiency** so that you are not wasting time or other resources. **Typically,** your steps will be in a **chronological**

order that gets you closer to your goal with the completion of each step. However, there may be circumstances that force you to have an irregular order that is not the most efficient and that's okay. While you don't have to put a timeframe on every step, timeframes do help you stay focused and keep you on track to achieve your goal.

Steps to Make an Action Plan

Step 1: Write out your goal. What do you want to do, to be, to have, or to achieve? Write a short, concise goal statement. If you need to break a large or difficult goal down into smaller steps, then state the smaller step (goal) you are going to work on.

Step 2: Make a list of all the tasks/steps/actions needed to achieve your goal. Your steps/actions should also be specific rather than described in detail. For example, describing the activity as "workout" is too broad. You need to **be specific**, like, "Workout or Lift weights: arm and back" or "Workout: row machine."

For more complicated goals, it may help you to **reverse engineer** the steps to **your goal**. Start at the end, that is, goal completion, and work backward, listing and describing what needs to occur in order to make each step happen.

Step 3: Rewrite your list of actions in the sequential order that best helps you reach your goal. Preferably, the order should be the most efficient order that maximizes the efficiency of your resources. However, there may be a specific order that is needed, and the most important task may need to be completed last rather than first. It's okay to have an irregular order as long as it moves you toward your goal achievement.

Step 4: Schedule a day and time allotted for each task/ step. Next to your listed activity, write the day, or week, and time you plan to do that action. So next to your activity of "Workout: row machine" you would add, "Tuesday, 30 minutes" or "Day 1, 30 to 60 minutes." If it's a once-a-week activity, then designate it as weekly.

If you are an **advanced planner** or **need more structure**, then you can **state the specific day, or date, and time of day** you plan to complete each step/activity. For example, "Tuesday (3/26), 5:00 a.m. to 5:30 a.m., instead of stating "30 minutes." Then **block** that **time out on your daily/weekly planner** and repeat this process for all your steps. This **advanced technique is called time blocking** and helps you with time management.

While you don't have to use a calendar, you should have a daily, weekly, and/or monthly schedule for each task until the goal is reached. **Making a schedule** and reviewing it **helps** you:

- **Stay on task** by telling what you need to do and when to do it.

- **Hold yourself accountable** for your time and effort.

- **Establish a routine**.

Step 5: Action! Start working on your 1st action/task and continue until it's completed. Then, start working on the 2nd action/ task, and so on.

Step 6: Measure/Document Your Activities by simply putting a check mark next to completed activities or writing down the actual number of completed activities like, **14 emails**, or **2 hours** on content creation.

Old School/Easy Action Plan

Take a sheet of paper, turn it longwise, and write your list of activities along the left margin. Then along the top, write the type of interval that best works for those activities, i.e.. Day-1/Week-1/Month-1. When you complete an action, you put a check mark under that day or write some type of measurement for that activity, like in Example 1 below. These example **Action Plans** are easy to incorporate into a **weekly planner/calendar**.

Example 1: Weekly Action Plan

Goal: I will weigh 190 lbs. on September 1, 2025.

Activity	Day-1	Day-2	Day-3	Day-4	Day-5	Day-6	Day-7
Meal prep:	1 hr			1 hr			Recover
Workout: weights, 5x5 routine		1 hr		1 hr		1 hr	
2 healthy meals/day	___	___	___	___	___	___	___
Workout: row/walk/ bike/core	30 min		30 min		30 min		

Results of Week 1: Weight: ____
Reward: Dessert

    To **keep track of your activities**, you can circle the times on the days you complete that activity or put check marks after them and on the empty lines for each healthy meal you eat.

    While it's not a requirement, you should **reward** yourself for success, so if you lost weight for the week, then you get a reward.

Keep it small and reasonable, but meaningful to you, like a certain dessert, a not-so-healthy meal, a movie, or a restaurant you want to try.

Example 2:

Goal: I will raise my sales to $10k per week by September 1, 2026.

Activity	Day-1	Day-2	Day-3	Day-4	Day-5	Day-6	Day-7
Initial emails to prospects	15/**14**	15/___	15/___	15/**20**	15/___		
Initial calls to prospects	15/___	15/**10**	15/___	15/___	15/**15**		
Follow-up emails to prospects	15/___	15/**12**	15/___	15/___	15/___		
Follow up calls to prospects-	**1**	__	**8**	__	**4**		

Other marketing, ex. social media, (Decide measurement, like time spent or # of posts)

Activity	Day-1	Day-2	Day-3	Day-4	Day-5	Day-6	Day-7
Content creation	1 hr	**1hr**	2 hr	____	____		
Service customers	1-2 hrs.		____	____	**2**	____	____

Sales Results for week _2_:
(Sales $ amount, or # of sales)

Just to clarify, 15 is your desired or ideal number of emails and calls to prospects, and the blank spaces next to the 15s are for you to write the actual number you completed.

Typically, your **Action Plan** is going to consist of daily and weekly activities. And it's in **following your plan** and **doing** those **Daily Activities** that

1. Lead you to accomplish your goal

2. Builds Discipline

3. Forms Habits

It's important to note that **you** can **be flexible** with your Action Plan should something unexpected occur and you need to **adjust your plan**. Also, it's important to keep **track** of your completed **activities** as you will need to **review/Monitor** your plan **weekly** or monthly to ensure that your activities are contributing to achieving your goal on time. The next chapter will cover the **Monitor** step.

I have included an example of a blank **Action Plan** in the Appendices section in the **back of** this **book**, or you can go to **icandream. net**, under Resources, for a link to downloadable Action Plans.

Vision without action is merely a dream.
Action without vision just passes the time.
Vision with action can change the world.

– Nelson Mandela

CHAPTER 9

Monitor: Your Progress and Make Course Corrections

*Stay committed to your decisions, but
stay flexible in your approach.*

– Tony Robbins

*Success comes from repeated efforts day in and day out. You
learn from your mistakes, make adjustments, and continue
pressing forward until you achieve the results you desire.*

– Zig Ziglar

You are the **CEO** of **YOUR life!** I think that's pretty important. Wouldn't you agree? While you can't control all the things around you or all the circumstances that occur in life, **you DO have** the **sole responsibility** and ultimate **power of HOW** you **respond**

to those circumstances. The last step of the **D.R.E.A.M. Method**, **Monitor**, is **how you** keep **watch** over **your** goal-achievement **progress** and **what** you do next.

STEP 5 OF THE D.R.E.A.M. GOAL-SETTING AND GOAL-ACHIEVEMENT METHOD IS MONITOR: YOUR PROGRESS AND MAKE COURSE CORRECTIONS.

You Monitor: Your Progress and Make Course Corrections by:

1. **Tracking completed tasks, activities, or steps** that you established in your Action Plan.

2. **Measuring** the **outcomes** of those **completed activities**.

3. **Evaluating** those **activities, outcomes, new information,** and any **other circumstances** that may affect your goal achievement.

4. **Making needed adjustments/corrections** to your Action Plan so you **stay on course** toward your **goal**.

Tracking Completed Activities

In his book, *The Courage to Succeed*, Ruben Gonzalez explained the importance of walking the luge track with his coach and taking notes as the coach described the peculiarities of each course and gave them valuable information. The activity wasn't just walking the track and looking, it was also taking notes and reviewing those notes, which helped Ruben navigate the course better, which meant faster, in the following days.

Ruben needed to get into the top 50 fastest times in the world to reach his goal of qualifying for the Olympics, so his run time on the luge track was his most important measurement. However, his other **activities,** like walking the track and working out, still needed to be **Monitored** and tracked, as they **built on each other** and contributed to his overall time improvement. That's why it's important to **Monitor** and **track** your **activities in addition to measuring** your **outcomes**.

Monitoring and Measuring Outcomes

Typically, you measure your progress by measuring the **outcomes of** your **activities**. In your **Action Plan**, most of your **Activities** should have some **specific measurements,** usually a **quantity** and/or **specific timeframe** that will **show your progress** toward your goal.

Also, you may have multiple timeframes in your Action Plan. Usually, you have **timeframes of days, weeks, or months** to keep track of scheduled activities and timeframes to show the **duration of an activity**.

Let's look at an **example** of a **completed Action Plan** and how to **Monitor** it. (You can visit **icandream.net** and get a blank copy of an Action Plan template.)

Example of Weekly Action Plan and Monitoring

Goal: to weigh **190 lbs.** by **9-1-2024. Week 3:**

Activity	Day-1	Day-2	Day-3	Day-4	Day-5	Day-6	Day-7
Meal prep:	1 hr-✓			1 hr-✓			Recover
Workout:							
weights, 5x5							
routine		1 hr ✓		1 hr ✓		1 hr ✓	
Two healthy							

meals/day	_ _ _	✓✓	_ ✓✓✓	✓✓	✓✓✓✓✓ ✓✓	_ _ _
<u>Activity</u>	Day-1	Day-2	Day-3	Day-4	Day-5 Day-6	Day-7
Workout: row/walk/ bike/core	30 min-✓		30 min-		30 min-✓	

Circle or put a check mark next to completed activities and for each daily, healthy meal you eat.

Results of 3rd week: Weight: <u>205 </u>
Reward: Ice cream

Weekly Measurements:
>   1. Days of exercise- <u>5</u>
>   2. Days w/ 2+ healthy meals- <u>5</u>
>   3. Meal preps – <u>2</u>
>   4. **Weight**- <u>205</u> lbs. (lost 2 lbs.)

Another Example of Monitoring Results is simply to write the specific measurements used to determine your progress toward your goal.

Day/**Week**/Month 1: Weigh- 200 lbs.
Day/**Week**/Month 3: Weigh- 195 lbs.
Day/Week/**Month** 2: No soda- 40 days
Day/Week/**Month** 4: Monthly sales- $20k

All this measuring may seem complicated, but it's really not. A simple check mark for completed activities will do. In short, you need to know if the steps/tasks/activities you are doing are moving you toward your goal or not.

Evaluating Your Progress

Next, you **evaluate** your **progress** toward your goal by **reviewing** your **completed activities** and their **outcomes**. Did you complete all of your activities? If not, **how many** or how **much** did you complete? If your outcomes were less than your weekly goals or what you expected, how much less? You need to **know** those **specific numbers** as they usually **explain why** you **made progress** toward your goal **or did not** make progress.

Looking at the **Week 3 Action Plan** above, your **Weekly Measurements** show you completed most of your scheduled activities. Also, your measured weight shows you made progress, which makes sense because you did the activities needed to help you lose weight.

Finally, you need to **evaluate** any other **factors** or **circumstances** that are affecting or may affect your progress. Did you discover any **new obstacles**? Did you have any **unexpected circumstances**, like you were sick for a day or two, resulting in you staying in bed and not completing any steps/activities that day? **Being aware** of these obstacles and/or circumstances **helps** you **understand** why you got the **results** you did and helps you **plan** accordingly.

This thought may be another "Captain Obvious" one, but I think it needs to be said: You need to **be** brutally **honest** with **yourself** in **Evaluating Your Progress**. Any **denial** of real **shortfalls** and **their causes** will only **result in denials** and **delays** in reaching your **goal**. Honest answers will help you clarify your situation and help you determine how to correct any issues.

Making Course Corrections

Let's say you evaluated your progress and determined that you are **not on track** to reach your goal. Unfortunately, you don't always get the results you want, even if you complete all of your activities. However, if this week is the 4th week in a row of not making a weekly goal, you need to **take** an **in-depth look** at why. When that occurs, you need to **review** your **activities, expected measurements, actual measurements**, and **timeframes.**

Were these activities, measurements, and timeframes **appropriate for your goal**? If not, then you might need to **adjust** one of them, like extending your goal due date or increasing an activity's duration. For example, that's why I used 30 minutes for the Walking/Rowing/Biking activity in the losing weight Action Plan example because, for me, doing those activities for only 20 minutes did not help me lose weight. For that reason, I made the small adjustment of increasing the time to 30 minutes, which did make a positive difference.

Usually, the **needed change** will be **obvious** and indicated by the **lower-than-expected results** of your outcomes. Again, those **honest answers** when evaluating are **necessary** and **important,** and you should know what step or activity has a shortfall. How far off from the expected measurement(s) were you? Maybe your weekly goal was not realistic. If you think your daily or weekly Activity outcome/goal is too high, then lower it. If one of your timeframes is too short, then make a **minor adjustment** to it. **Start with small adjustments** so you can better understand and control the effects of your changes.

Your best guess on what to change will be good enough. And if, in another week or month, you need to adjust the same step or a different activity, **don't worry** about making a **mistake**; just make the change. You **know your situation** and your plan the best. Whatever the case may be, just **make** the **needed course correction** and start doing it. **Don't quit, just make adjustments**.

Also, **consider** your **overall timeline** and **due date** for your goal. If you are working on a long-term goal, with a due date over a year away, and you only have a few weeks of shortfalls, I don't think you need to change your due date. Evaluating and changing one of your activities might be necessary and more helpful. Usually, a minor change is all that's needed.

Persistent Problems

Like many people, there came a time in my life when I needed to lose weight. I had been an athlete all my life, playing a variety of sports. In high school, I ran cross-country and track, and continued running as an exercise until I turned 40 and developed constant knee pain. In the Army, I was a physical fitness stud, always finishing with one of the top scores for our physical fitness tests if not the top. Even when I could no longer run, I still exercised and tried to eat healthy.

However, getting older, adulting, and a sedentary job snuck up on me and shoved a bunch of chocolate chip cookies down my throat and around my waist. When my health issues started occurring more and more, I knew I needed to lose some weight. I knew how to exercise and eat healthy, so off I went trying to lose that weight. However, I did not write my weight goal down, at least not at first, and I did not make an Action Plan or keep track of activities. I had my goal in my mind and knew what I needed to do.

Despite my efforts, I still wasn't losing weight, and my health/ overweight issues continued. It was during the time I was writing this book so I applied the **D.R.E.A.M. Method** to my goal. At the time, I weighed 213 pounds. My goal was to weigh 190 pounds. In my **Step 2**, **Resources,** shown in Chapter 6, I listed my friend Troy as a Resource because he was an Ironman (triathlon) competitor and an avid weightlifter since high school.

Yes, I was a little embarrassed and reluctant to call him at first because that meant admitting I, the "athlete," needed help, but phys- ical pain is a good motivator. Also, I wasn't going to let pride stop me from achieving my goal. When I called him and **discussed** my weight **goal** and the **Obstacles** I was facing, he was happy to help.

While I considered myself knowledgeable about diet and exercise, I knew I could **always learn more**. After talking with my friend, I realized that there was a lot more I needed to learn, and our conversation **confirmed** the **value** of a **coach** or **mentor**. First, he helped me realize that while I was lifting weights, I was not doing enough sets. Second, most weight loss or gain at our age, over 50, was diet-related, and there was more I needed to know and things to change about my diet. Based on his advice and guidance, I made a few small adjustments to my Action Plan, and it worked. I lost 20 pounds in less than three months and got down to 193 pounds.

While I didn't get to my goal of 190, I was able to stay around 193 lbs., so I considered my efforts successful as I felt and looked better. Those results were based on that Action Plan and those activities. To lose more weight, I would have to make further adjustments to my Action Plan. My **success** only **came after** I got **help from an expert**, my fitness coach.

So, if you are making adjustments and still not finding a solution, then you may need to **consult** with a **mentor, coach**, or some **other professional** to help you solve an issue. Maybe one of your peers who does, or did, the same job can review the problem for you. Also, don't forget to review your **Resources**, as you may have listed someone who can help you. If **problems persist**, it's time to reach out for **help**.

Another **tactic for persistent problems** is that you may have to **approach** the **problem**/shortfall as a **new goal**. If so, then **go through the D.R.E.A.M. process** for that particular problem. It may delay your main goal, but sometimes these changes are necessary to overcome problems and for your goal achievement. **You CAN overcome** problems.

Review and Adjust

Even if you are on track to achieving your goal, you should **review** your **progress regularly** and **evaluate** what's working, what isn't, and what may work better. Then, **after your evaluation, make adjustments**.

After-Action Reviews

After achieving your goal, **review** your **Action Plan** to see what **worked well**, what **didn't** work, and what you **can improve** for **future** Action Plans and goals. These types of after-action reviews are used in the military all the time. Make notes about your findings so you can review them in the future if needed. Then, apply what you learned to your next goal.

Reward Yourself

Once you accomplish your goal, it is time to **reward yourself.** You should not skip this step. In addition to the **small weekly rewards,** at the end of your Action Plan, you should have a final, significant **Reward listed**. Rewarding yourself for your accomplishments is **positive reinforcement,** which will subconsciously program your mind to want to achieve more, so **celebrate** and **enjoy your achievements.**

Goals You Can't Measure

Certain goals, like **Personal Growth** goals of **Spirituality** or being more **Mindful**, really won't have specific measurements and outcomes that show your progress. However, you can still make an Action Plan and keep **track** of **activities** that you think contribute to your success for that goal.

For example, for a goal of being more **Mindful**, you can keep track of the number of times a day or just days that you said please and thank you to people, or that you smiled and made eye contact when greeting people. There are quite a few activities to consider and that you can keep track of for goals like being more Mindful or Spirituality, but your progress and certainly your achievement of those goals will be your own judgment based on how you feel or think. Again, **you're the CEO** of You, so **it's up to you**.

In summary, **Monitoring Your Progress helps** you determine:

1. **Your progress** or lack of progress toward your goal.
2. **What activities are helping** you move toward your goal and which ones aren't.
3. **What areas you can improve** and if you need to make **corrections** or **adjustments** to your Action Plan.

Monitoring also helps you **stay connected** to your Goals and **motivated** by **showing** your **progress** and giving you **positive reinforcement** with small rewards.

When it is obvious that the goals cannot be reached,
don't adjust the goals, adjust the action steps.

– Author unknown

CHAPTER 10

Don't Listen to The Haters: Overcoming Obstacles

"I'm not going to limit myself just because people won't accept the fact that I can do something else."

–Dolly Parton

"… your worst enemy is fear."

– Mahatma Gandhi

A GOOD GIRL IN A BAD WORLD

In 1970, Lois was 20 years old, living alone, and working for an insurance company in California. The apartments she lived in were nice and had top security with key cards for the garage and buildings with professors and doctors living there. One evening, when a man knocked on her door claiming to be a neighbor, she opened her door without hesitation.

It was a stranger who immediately rushed in, grabbed her throat with both hands, and started choking her. The man kicked the door closed, pushed her back, and continued to strangle and sexually assault her for 30 minutes or longer. During the assault, while going in and out of consciousness, Lois believed she was going to be killed. Despite the prolonged strangulation and being left bloody and bruised, she survived the horrific attack. However, the damage was done.

Lois was so traumatized and scared that she didn't leave her apartment for two weeks and literally began to starve. At that time, Lois was also a part-time model and a dancer on *The Real Don Steal Show* filmed on Hollywood Blvd. Like many rape victims, she thought the police would not believe her or would blame her for the attack because she was "sexy," so she did not report the crime.

Making matters worse, both her boyfriend and best friend had recently moved out of state, leaving Lois completely alone with no one to confide in. She felt like she couldn't tell anyone else, so she didn't. She didn't even admit to herself that it happened for six years.

Lois wanted to help people and use her talents, so the following year she moved to Texas and started college to become a maxillofacial prosthesis technician. This detailed training gave her in-depth knowledge of skull structure. In addition, to make some extra money, she began drawing fine-art portraits of tourists on the River Walk in San Antonio, where she completed over 3,000 pastel portraits. She didn't know it at the time, but **her formal education** and **experience drawing** portraits had **given her** some **very special skills.**

In 1982, now living in Houston, Lois and a friend saw a news report about the rape of a dance instructor in front of her students. Lois **believed** she could **draw** the **suspect from descriptions** given by the little girls who witnessed the crime. To **test her theory**, Lois had her friend go to the corner gas station and look at the man working there. When her friend returned, Lois sketched the man from her friend's description. Then, they went to the gas station and looked. Her sketch was almost exact. She realized then that **she could draw people she hadn't seen before.**

Later that year, Lois, despite her self-doubt, contacted the police department multiple times and tried to explain what she could do. She got **transferred around** from division to division and was initially met with **repeated rejection** and even **hostile opposition**. At first, **they didn't understand** what she wanted to do. Many Detectives simply **did not believe** that she could make a sketch of the suspect that could lead to the suspect's identification. **Those People's limiting beliefs did affect Lois, causing her to have doubts about herself and her skills.**

Don't Listen to Those People—The Haters

However, **Lois did not give up. She believed** that she could help. She knew better than most people, even more than most police officers, the kind of monsters that are out there. One by-product of her attack was that it gave her courage, so **she called again** and finally **got a detective lieutenant to agree to a demonstration.**

For this demonstration, they sent a secretary, their "witness", to look at someone in the jail. Then, sitting in the lieutenant's office with her back to the door and a bunch of detectives crowded around watching, the drawing took shape as **Lois sketched** the **suspect** from the **secretary's description.** They were blown away. **She nailed it, a match.**

A Forensic Sketch Artist is Born

After her demonstration, several detectives **gave Lois a chance,** and she did a few sketches. Then, a month or so later, she did her first sketch for a homicide case. The witness was hysterical, and

Lois had to handle their trauma to get the information out of them for the sketch. Afterward, Lois **felt mentally exhausted**. She also **had self-doubts** about the quality of her sketch and thought she would not do that again.

The next day she was contacted by the homicide detective who told her to come down and see him. Once there, he said, "**You did it!**" Lois didn't understand what he meant at first. The detective told her they showed her sketch on TV, and the killer's roommate called and turned him in, which led to a search and recovery of the murder weapon. He told her that they **would not have solved the case** if she had not done the sketch. It took several minutes for it all to sink in, but then she realized that **her sketch** had just **solved a murder.**

Lois described that **feeling** as one of the **best in the world.** She was hooked. She had **found her purpose** through her **passion.** For less than an hour of work, which really wasn't working for her, she could **put a monster behind bars**. Just by doing something she **enjoyed, sketching**, she could **help someone get** the **justice** she never got. Her new "work" also **served as** a kind of **therapy** that she needed. **Helping others helped her** deal with and heal from her own trauma.

Then, more and more detectives, including other law enforcement agencies, started using her skills. She continued sketching with positive results for decades. Throughout her almost 40-year career in law enforcement, Lois did **thousands of sketches** with a **30% identification success rate**. While 30% may not seem very high, it is **very successful, considering those were cases with zero percent** of means to identify the suspect. Those were cases where the suspect's identification was not known, and there were no videos or photos of the suspect.

By the end of her career, Lois's sketches led to the identification and arrest of **over 1,300 suspects.** Those suspects were the worst.

They were **kidnappers, robbers, rapists, and murderers**. Lois's work also **brought justice to many victims** and gave them and their **families closure**. In addition, her work has also helped exonerate several wrongfully accused persons and helped identify the real suspects.

Best in The World

In 2017, the ***Guinness Book of World Records* recognized Lois Gibson as the most successful Forensic Artist in the World.** Lois' talent has taken her to the FBI National Academy, and all around the World, teaching and sharing her knowledge and skills. And her success continued until she retired in 2021. Pretty impressive for a good girl from Kansas.

Throughout her **life** and **career**, Lois faced all sorts of **obstacles**. She had to face and **overcome** her own fears, roadblocks, and limiting beliefs, starting with her brutal sexual assault and attempted murder at just 20 years of age. Then, she had to face and deal with other people's fears and limiting beliefs just so she could help solve horrible crimes and help victims. Even with the success of her sketches, she continued to face various obstacles and challenges within the police department. But again, and again, **she did not give up.**

OBSTACLES

I shared Lois' story because, like her, **you** too will **face obstacles** of all kinds throughout your life, especially in the pursuit of your goals. You will come across people who do not believe in you or possibly just do not believe in your goal. And it's **those people**, the **haters,** the **doubters**, the **non-believers**, the negative knuckleheads, that can **purposely or inadvertently** stop or **kill your** desires and **goals**.

Those People's incorrect, limiting beliefs are **Obstacles**. Unfortunately, those types of Obstacles are **common**, and we face them and an assortment of other obstacles in everyday life. **We** also **create obstacles for ourselves** through self-doubt, procrastination, our comfort zones, negative self-talk, and others.

Obstacles are **things** that are **in our way**. They can be external or physical obstacles or internal, or rather, mental obstacles. Concerning goal achievement, obstacles are more **commonly mental,** and the **biggest obstacle is our own minds**. And if you do not know how to address or handle obstacles properly, they **can be goal killers.**

Consequently, you need to **know** what **obstacles** you are facing and **how** to **overcome** them. **Obstacles** come in the form of **Limiting Beliefs, Fears, Roadblocks, and Other Hazards.** I will explain each one, and then explain how to overcome them. I know there is a lot of in-depth information, so if you find yourself losing interest, then, at least, read the major categories and skim the paragraph titles for subjects of interest. You also **don't** want to **miss** the **Secrets.**

Limiting Beliefs

Limiting beliefs are **false beliefs** that **dictate** or **limit behavior** in some way. These obstacles **can be** in the form of Our Own Limiting Beliefs or the Limiting Beliefs of Others. It's our beliefs that **put boundaries** on our **thoughts** and **actions**. However, **most** of our beliefs are **taught** to us by others, at least when we are young. Sometimes these **beliefs give** us **boundaries** that are **good** when they keep us from doing wrong or unsafe things. **Other times**, they hold us back from accomplishing goals.

Limiting Beliefs of Others

While our self-imposed limits are the hardest to overcome, the **Limiting Beliefs of Others** are also **very impactful** as they are the beliefs and thoughts of our **family, friends,** and **society.**
Has someone ever said to you:

- You can't do that
- You're dreaming
- You're too young to do that
- You're too old to do that
- You're too (<u>whatever</u>)
- You're not smart enough
- That's too hard for you
- They are keeping you down
- Why don't you be a _____ instead of trying to be a _____ (fill in with your dream job/occupation)?

And the **biggest limiting belief** of all, **"That's impossible."**

These are all examples of the **limiting beliefs of others** that are **transferred to us** through **learned behavior.** The problem is that **most of us accept** these beliefs as the truth, or what is correct or acceptable, or what is possible or not possible. **Why?** Because it's our **family, friends, community, and our society that taught them to us.**

Many times, we are inadvertently taught limiting beliefs as a child to "protect" us from emotional difficulties. For example, the saying, "Don't get your hopes up about ___(fill in the blank with something you want) because you don't want to be disappointed." While the intent is to help or protect the person, the result is the spread and continuation of a limiting belief. So yes, you can blame your parents for some of your problems. However, you can only do that for so long. At some point, **you must take responsibility for your own thoughts and actions**.

So, What is the Harm?

The harm is that most limiting beliefs are **based on false, incorrect, or partially incorrect information.** As a result, people's **actions** or **inactions** are **based** on this **false information**. In addition, these **learned behaviors can spread limiting beliefs** like a disease. We don't realize we have the condition, so we continue the same behaviors and pass on our limiting beliefs and practices to others, and the cycle continues.

Most racism, sexism, or any other **prejudices** or biases are **learned behaviors**, and their **effects** can be **devastating** and lasting to an individual and our society as a whole. People's lives and our society are not going to be better when people's thoughts and actions are based on false or incorrect information.

Our Own Limiting Beliefs

Sadly, our **parents, family, friends,** and **society** are still **teaching us** many **limiting beliefs,** which can weigh us down emotionally and create unnecessary mental barriers. Just the thought of goal planning can overwhelm some people as they think it's some complicated tasks, and most people don't want complicated or hard. When faced with difficult tasks, or perceived as difficult, people revert to the limiting beliefs they heard from others, and we tell ourselves the same things.

Have you ever said to yourself or someone else about yourself:

- I can't do that

- I'm just dreaming about that

- I'm too young

- I'm too old

- I'm not smart enough

- I'm not good enough

- That's too hard for me

- Maybe I should just be a _______ instead of trying to be a ____ (fill in with your dream job/occupation)

And still the **biggest limiting belief** of all, **"That's impossible."** These same **limiting beliefs of others get passed on** and **become our own** limiting beliefs. Our own self-imposed boundaries based on false beliefs can also end up killing our dreams and goals.

*** SECRET ***

The biggest and most difficult obstacles to achieving any of our goals are our own limiting beliefs.

Fortunately, **you can throw off learned behaviors**, prejudices, biases, and limiting beliefs, by simply believing, **I CAN!** Lois first believed that she couldn't make a difference or help herself by speaking up, but then she realized she could and made a difference to thousands of people. The only thing that stood in her way was a limiting belief. What limiting beliefs are standing in your way? If you thought of one, then it's time to overcome it.

Fears

Fears and **doubts** are **common emotional responses** to experiences or beliefs. Some of the most frequent obstacles that cause us to **miss opportunities** or that stop us from achieving our goals are Fears. Most times, our fears are **not based on** the true **reality** of the situation. Hence the **F.E.A.R. acronym, False Evidence Appearing Real**.

However, the **negative effects of Fears** are **very real** and can be **dream- and goal-killers**. In my experience and observations, it's Fears that **stop people from even starting** on a goal, and it stops them from continuing when a difficult situation occurs.

These are the **most common Fears** that keep people from achieving their goals.

Fear of the Unknown

Life brings change, and some changes are uncomfortable. The **biggest stressor** for most people is fear of the **unknown,** which often occurs during changes in our lives. **Not knowing what is going to happen** next, or what to expect, and the **build-up of anticipation** that occurs, can literally make people sick.

Fear of Failure

Fear of Failure is a fear of **failing** at something we attempt. No one wants to feel embarrassed or disappointed, and those are feelings we usually experience when we try something and fail at it. Failure also opens us up to the judgment of others, which is another situation everyone wants to avoid. This fear **causes** us to **avoid or delay** doing the very activities that could help us be successful, and it stops many people from even getting started on a goal.

Fear of Rejection

Fear of Rejection is a fear of **you or your ideas not being liked** or accepted by others. It's the fear of asking **someone** for something and them **telling you "No."** No one likes being rejected or not liked, even for something small. This fear **is paralyzing** for many people because you can't control other people's responses, and it's very **hard for people to not take rejection personally**.

Fear of Success

Fear of Success is a **fear** of the **consequences** or **changes** or the potential for these changes that come with being successful. For example, if you achieve something difficult, then people will expect you to do it again.

Fear of Change a.k.a. The Comfort Zone

This fear has been **my nemesis**. My **Comfort Zone** is sitting on my big, blue, comfy couch watching TV. I am totally **content and safe**. I'm happy both physically and mentally. So why the heck would I want to leave that comfort zone except to get another drink or snack?

Why do reasonably intelligent people like you and me **choose not to do** something that would benefit us? The answer: **Fear of Change**. Fear of Change is a **fear** of facing **new experiences** or **situations**. New things and **changes** to our **current situation equals unknown** situations, and that **equals anxiety** and **fears**.

We think it's good to protect ourselves and stay safe, be it physically or mentally. In fact, our brains are programmed to conserve energy, and they like the usual routine and dislike change.

Our **Comfort Zones** are the nice, warm, safe places where we are **protected from** the **harshness** or perceived harshness **of reality**. It's our comfortable **daily routines** where we know exactly what is going to happen. There are **no surprises**. It's where you don't have to exert much effort, and you know what your reward will be.

We all **feel safe** and **protected** in our comfort zones, and who doesn't like feeling safe? It's an easy formula: if you don't go outside of your Comfort Zone, then you **don't get rejected**, you **don't face the unknown**, you **don't feel uncomfortable**, and you **don't fail**.

Or so You Thought

The **truth** is, while the **Comfort Zone keeps you safe**, it also **keeps you unsuccessful**. It **limits** your **opportunities** and **experiences,** keeping you from becoming a better version of yourself. So, if you **want to grow** significantly, if you want to take steps that will change your life for the better, you will need to **step outside** of the protection of your **comfort zone**.

Other Fears/Phobias

There are too many fears and phobias that affect people to properly address them all in this book. **Social Phobia,** also called Social Anxiety Disorder**,** is a **fear** of being in common **social situations**, which I think is so common in younger generations, it is a frequent characteristic of those generations. I understand, no one wants to feel awkward or embarrassed, especially in front of others.

Roadblocks

While people often refer to mental barriers as roadblocks, **for the D.R.E.A.M Method, Roadblocks are actual physical obstacles** that **stand in the way** of you reaching your goals, or **something** physical that you need that **you are lacking**. Some examples would be a **lack of money, or a piece of equipment used** for your business **breaks** down.

Remember the driving across the US goal example. Roadblocks could include a road closure, a traffic jam, or running out of gas. You **can anticipate** and **plan for Roadblocks**, but sometimes they happen unexpectedly. **If** they are **unexpected, then** you simply **evaluate** the new circumstances and **make** the necessary **adjustments** to your Action Plan.

In planning for Roadblocks, some of the items on your **Resources You Need** list **may be Roadblocks**. And that's okay. If you know you need something, then you can plan on how to get it. **Addressing a Roadblock may need to be the first step in your Action Plan**. Being aware of an issue and being able to address it is always better than not knowing.

Other Hazards

Hazards cover several **different types of obstacles** that you need to be aware of. These obstacles can be internal or external and include things like **misinformation, negativity,** and **other mind traps**.

Misinformation

Misinformation is **false or misleading information** and can **cause** you to **waste time, energy,** and **other resources.** In today's world, with information and advice for everything at your fingertips, how do you know what advice or information is right or truthful?

Sadly, false or misleading information has become a major problem in society today. Some of the largest and most popular social media platforms, mainstream news outlets, and search engines censor information and people they disagree with, and they flat-out disregard the truth and promote lies instead. Also, people's self-interest and greed, especially for money, often overrules the truth and doing the right thing. As a result, people can compromise information sources.

The 1953 Yale and 1979 Harvard Goal Studies

For example, for years many popular self-help experts referenced **the 1953 Yale and 1979 Harvard goal studies,** which is how I first heard the information. Those goal studies claimed that by simply writing down your goal, a person was 50% more likely to achieve that goal. While those claims seemed reasonable, it turned out the studies never happened. Those references and claims were essentially **false information**.

So please verify your facts and sources so that you are not an accidental co-conspirator and promoter of **false information.**

FOMO and The Shiny Penny Syndrome

People like **new things,** be it objects or ideas, and marketers use this fact against us. They use popular **"gurus"** and **"experts"** to say this **new technique** or system **is the best** and will **solve** all **your problems,** and make people feel they **must buy it, now,** with sayings like, "This special offer is today only" or "Ends at midnight." They **appeal** to your Fear of Missing Out (**FOMO**) with their advertisement, and **Bam! You've bought** or tried something else that you probably don't need. Sound familiar? Don't worry, you're not alone. It happens to all of us.

Modeling

Modeling is usually a positive and very effective technique. Modeling is simply **copying** or following **another person's actions or behaviors** to get the same or similar result. The idea of **Modeling** is to model the behaviors of successful people who have already accomplished the goal you want to achieve.

I mention it as a Hazard because while **you can model someone's behavior** or specific actions and produce similar results, you **can't model someone's exact thoughts, beliefs, emotions, experiences, or motivation,** i.e., their starting situation. Therefore, you **shouldn't expect** to produce the **exact, same results**. That's why you have to establish your own goals and your own Action Plan, or path, to achieve them.

Comparing

Comparing **is expecting the same results** as the person you were **Modeling,** or **comparing your outcomes to someone else's** outcome. Comparing is not a good thing to do. I think everyone can remember a time when they compared themselves to someone else. Maybe it was in school, in sports, or at work, but **we often compare our** own **successes or failures to others,** and that is a **mistake**. Yes, you studied, you practiced, or you worked hard, and then, some other person performed better than you or was recognized for their efforts, and you weren't.

Welcome to Life! Sometimes life is unfair, or unkind, or just not right, or all of the above, and it makes you want to scream or cry. I get it. If you need to, go ahead and scream or have a good cry. Then get up, get back on your horse, or bicycle, or electric scooter, and **get back to working on your goal. Failures, setbacks, and challenges are just other steps on the road to your goal**, and sometimes you must take those steps as well, even if they are unpleasant or you don't like them.

Negativity

Negativity is having a bad, gloomy, pessimistic, or complaining attitude towards things. Like Limiting Beliefs, these Obstacles **can be our own or someone else's**. Also, like Limiting Beliefs, Negativity is often a **learned behavior** and **can be spread** to others. We've all been around those Debbie or Danny Downer people who find the worst in every situation. And if you continue to stay around those people or that kind of environment, it will eventually affect you, negatively.

OVERCOMING OBSTACLES

Obstacles will occur. They will come in all shapes, sizes, and manners—big, small, difficult, easy, or barely noticeable. After reading the descriptions of all those Obstacles, did you find any that you experienced or are currently experiencing? If not, great. If yes, then as previously stated, you need to know how to properly address and overcome those Obstacles, or they can end up stopping your goal achievement.

There are **3 steps to Overcoming All Obstacles**:

1. Acknowledge
2. Identify
3. Take Action

How to Overcome Obstacles

First, you need to **acknowledge** that the **Obstacle exists** or can exist. Ignoring it will not make it go away. Also, you can't pass the blame of any obstacle or failure onto anyone or anything else. Your past or current situation up until today may be the product mostly of other people's actions, like your learned behaviors, but **starting right NOW, your future** and **how you respond** and **handle** Obstacles or issues is **solely up to you**.

***** SECRET *****

If you want to be successful, you must take ownership of your thoughts, actions, and situation.

Second, once you acknowledge that an **Obstacle** exists, you need to **identify the Obstacle**. Knowing what specific obstacle is affecting you will help you determine the best way to overcome it. **Road-blocks** or physical obstacles, like a literal traffic jam or getting sick, causing you to have to stay in bed, identify themselves, while some **Limiting Beliefs and Fears** may be harder to identify. To **help you identify** or **define** the Obstacle, you may need to ask yourself a few questions such as:

- What do I think or feel is the problem or obstacle?

- Are there any actions or steps I am avoiding?

- Are there any actions or steps that I'm not giving my full effort on?

Write out your answers. Seeing words can help trigger other thoughts and words that can **help** you **identify** and **define** your **Obstacle**. Also, by writing your Obstacle down, you are officially

acknowledging it, which will allow you to **better address it**.

If you can't quite identify your Obstacle, that's where **coaches, mentors**, or **friends can help** you. They may be able to immediately tell you exactly what the problem/obstacle is. If not, then they can work with you and help you identify it.

*** SECRET ***

Advice from coaches and mentors on how to plan for, avoid, or handle an Obstacle can be invaluable. A coach telling you **what NOT to do** can be just as valuable as them telling you what to do.

Finally, Destroy Your Obstacle!

Once you **identify** your **Obstacle, you need to Take Action** and **destroy it**. I know some of you are thinking —Ron, why all the violence? Because that Obstacle is **in the way of your Goal**, your **Success**, your **Freedom**, your **Happiness.** Your goals and success are worth the blood, sweat, and tears that it may take, or is taking, to achieve them, so you need to have a "destroy that obstacle" mentality when they are preventing your success. Having the right mentality when confronting Obstacles makes all the difference in the world, which means having and continuing with your **I Can! belief and attitude.**

*** SECRET ***

You destroy and Overcome Obstacles by taking action.

Once you identify the obstacle, usually, one or two obvious actions to address the problem come to mind. For example, you identify your Fear of Failure as what is keeping you from applying for a certain job. You know you can take action by practicing a job interview in front of a mirror or with a friend. The action(s) you take to help can be small. If the obstacle is big and/or complex with many actions to take, you **may need to make it a new goal and apply the D.R.E.A.M. process to it.** Try the correction you think of first and see if that works. If it doesn't, then **use** the **Monitoring step process** to address the Obstacle.

OVERCOMING LIMITING BELIEFS

Overcoming the Limiting Beliefs of Others, aka the Haters or Those People

I'm a part of 10% to 12% of the World's population that, through a natural genetic variation, ends up with a certain condition. Unfortunately, for me and the other hundreds of millions of people that fall into this group, the **majority of people** in the world **don't like us** because of our condition. They think we are more likely to:

- have more mental health problems

- die earlier

- more likely to be considered poor

- be criminals, evil, or witches

- and until relatively recently, in one modern country, was considered a valid reason to divorce this type of person.

So, what group are you thinking of? Did a particular race, ethnicity, religious, or political group come to mind? Well, it's not any of those. The horrible and dastardly group that I'm a part of and that I'm talking about is, of course, left-handed people. Yes, **left-handed** people. Seriously. I'm not making this up.

There was an article in Smithsonian.com from May 17, 2013, by Rose Eveleth, titled "Two-Thirds of the World Still Hate Lefties". The article stated that 2/3 of the world's left-handed population still face discrimination in the Middle East, Africa, India, Asia, and many other countries. Even in countries that are considered modern, the evidence of left-handed discrimination persists in culture, in language, thought, and cultural design. Sadly, there are enough examples to write an entire book on the discrimination of left-handers just using modern-day examples.

So how do you overcome the **Limiting Beliefs of Others, a.k.a. the Haters or Those People,** even when the others are your **family,** your **friends,** and your **society**? That's easy, you **do not listen to the Haters or Those People.** Just remember there are **billions,** not millions, **billions** of **people** in the World, including your family, friends, and your community, **with limiting beliefs,** and most are **unaware** of **how ridiculous their beliefs are** or how they got them. That may sound kind of mean, but it's the truth of the situation. So do not let someone else's uneducated, small, or limited mind stop you from achieving your goals. You will not and cannot please everyone not matter what you do, so don't try. Simply walk around them, climb over, or drive on by.

Sometimes the journey to your goal is lonely. Other people may not believe in you or your goal or care about your success. When those situations occur, you may need to remove yourself, at least temporarily, from those people, even if they are people you care about. Your goals and your happiness are worth it.

You **overcome** the **Limiting Beliefs of Others by**:

- Going through the 3 steps to Overcoming All Obstacles.

- Having an **I Can!** belief and attitude.

- Knowing that **you determine your future**, not others.

- Accepting that many **people** are **unaware** of **their own limiting beliefs**, and you don't have to listen to them and probably shouldn't.

- Knowing most of the time, **the Haters** and **Those People care more about themselves than you**, so they will speak and act in their best interest, not yours.

- Knowing that other **people's judgments** of you often reflect their own **insecurities**.

- **Taking actions** that move you toward your goal.

Overcoming Your Own Limiting Beliefs

Remember the question, what beliefs are standing in your way? Overcoming Your Own Limiting Beliefs is harder than Overcoming the Limiting Beliefs of Others because **changing yourself** is the **hardest** thing to **change**. However, you can overcome them in much the same way by **using** the **Three Steps** to Overcome All Obstacles.

Start by being **honest** with yourself: **admit** there is a **problem** or obstacle, or at least acknowledge the possibility of one, and **identify it**. **Then,** you **take the necessary action** to overcome the obstacle.

Information is your friend, so look for it and **gather facts**. Educate yourself about limiting beliefs and other obstacles by reviewing the ones in this book. Look for real world examples to prove yourself right or wrong about that belief. **You want the truth** on the matter. For example, your limiting belief: "I'm too old." Proof against that limiting belief is KFC founder Colonel Sanders was 64 years old before he hit success. Also, most people don't become millionaires until they are in their 50s. There are people in their 80s and 90s running marathons, getting their high school diplomas, and getting college degrees. So, your **limiting belief of "I'm too old" is not true**.

Sometimes the **problem** is only **our perception** of the situation. Meaning, in reality, there is no problem; **it's only in our head**. It's like **when other people judge you. It's usually a reflection of their own insecurities**, and the only problem is in their head. Just realize that you may have limiting beliefs that you need to overcome. **You do you** and keep your **I Can! belief** and attitude.

OVERCOMING FEARS

How Do We Overcome Fears?

Again, use the 3 steps to Overcoming All Obstacles, and **acknowledge, identify, and take action** on **your obstacle/fear**. You can more easily fix or solve a problem or issue once you are aware of and identify it. In addition, it's hard to overcome a general fear of a situation or some other general issue, which is why you need to **specifically define your fear**. The easiest way to define a fear is by **writing it out**. This way you officially acknowledge the issue which will allow you to better address it. Also, know it's ok to call it a fear, or problem, or issue. Again, having issues and fears is common and just part of life.

Like any obstacle, or situation, the more information you have about it, the better off you will be when deciding the best action to take. So, **educate yourself** on that **fear**. What is it? What does it mean? Is it the actual issue? Then, **decide what action** or actions **to take**, and **take them**. Also, know that doing something different may not change your situation. Meaning, you may take an action to overcome a fear, and it may not work. Your fear may remain. However, the fact that you tried, i.e. took action, to address your fear means that **you can do something** about it. So even if a fear is not eliminated, hopefully, its effects on you are decreased.

Also**, learn from your failures**, or mistakes, and **apply that experience** to your next plan and **take the next action** or step. And repeat this step as many times as needed. As previously mentioned, you may need to make overcoming the obstacle its own goal. If needed, then do it. No big deal.

OVERCOMING ROADBLOCKS

Roadblocks are actual **physical obstacles** that stand in the way of you reaching your goals. Often the **thought** of an obstacle, be it a Fear or a **Roadblock**, is **worse than** the **reality.** Like when you're driving on the freeway, and you come up on stopped cars in front of you. Often, our minds tend to think the worst. You think what if it's some major car crash and the freeway is closed. We think the delay will be long, but then we see a car pulling off the freeway and the delay/Roadblock is over. And all we needed to overcome the Roadblock was a few seconds or a few minutes of patience.

Roadblocks are typically the easiest obstacles to identify and overcome as they can be anticipated and then addressed in your Action Plan. When they arise, you simply **adjust your Action Plan** to address them immediately if needed, or at the appropriate time.

OVERCOMING OTHER HAZARDS

When you are on your road to your goal, you can certainly expect some unknown or uncomfortable changes. What you do when you come across those situations will determine your success or failure in reaching your goals.

These Obstacles can **cause you to lose focus** on the task/goal you are currently working toward. Your motivation may be to find a better or faster way to reach your goal, but what usually ends up happening is that you find that special information or person, or that shiny object, is not that special, and you've wasted more time and resources. So, **stay focused** on your goal and your goal achievement method/system, preferably the **D.R.E.A.M. Method**.

These Hazards were previously discussed in the Other Hazards section with some mention of tactics to overcome them, so here are brief recaps of **how to overcome** these **common Hazards.**

Overcoming Misinformation

Do your own **research** and **verify** information. Also, use multiple sources when researching and obtaining information. If you're doing an internet search, often the first several responses and sometimes the entire first page are paid advertisements.

Overcoming The Shiny Penny Syndrome and FOMO

Stay focused on achieving your goal and following your goal achievement method/system, preferably the **D.R.E.A.M. Method**. You can always try the latest and greatest thing after you achieve your goal.

Overcoming Modeling

Remember, you can't model someone's exact thoughts, beliefs, emotions, experiences, or motivation, i.e., their starting situation. Therefore, you **shouldn't expect** to produce the **exact same results**. **Establish your** own **goals** and **your** own **Action Plan**, or path, to reach your goals. You can model proven actions, but cherish and emphasize your uniqueness in those actions.

Overcoming Comparing

There are too many variables to accurately compare between two people and two situations. Remember, everyone has their own starting situation and unique route to their goal. Yes, sometimes **life is unfair**, and you may not always receive fair treatment. Failures, setbacks, and challenges are just other steps on **your road** to **your goal**, so **focus on your performance** and **your uniqueness. You do you**, not someone else.

Overcoming Your Negativity

If you find yourself being **Negative** about a goal, task, or situation, ask yourself why. Is there **any valid reason** why I can't accomplish what I want to accomplish? Or is your negativity about the task really a fear? If you think of something, **write it down**. Then, **write down ways** or actions you can take **to overcome** this obstacle. Now, you have a new goal and an action plan. Then, take action.

Overcoming Others' Negativity

If you find yourself in a situation with negative people or circumstances, the easiest solution is to **remove yourself**. Just leave and go home, go to your bedroom, go for a walk, go exercise.

If you are at work or in a situation where you can't leave, then the solution may be harder. You may have to listen to someone vent their frustration and talk negatively. It may be your boss. But I would take a situation like this as an **opportunity to offer help or assistance** to that person. You **never know when someone really needs help,** and they will remember your kindness.

I know, you are saying, "Hey, you just told us to remove ourselves from the negativity." However, when it comes to **personal or work relationships**, then you need to **consider the whole situation**. If people are just standing around bashing other people, then yes, just leave. But if someone comes to you with an issue and is being negative, then I would suggest you consider listening. They may want your advice, or see you as a reliable person or just want to see how you handle a situation. Listening and being courteous won't hurt you, and it may give you the opportunity to provide a positive influence on the situation.

Also, be aware of the negativity from TV, social media, or any other source of negative news. Turn them off and find a source that is positive. There are too many choices available, so do not subject yourself to negativity.

Is Overcoming Obstacles really that simple?

Yes, it can be. It can be as **easy or** as **hard** as you want to make it. **You Can and Do decide**. So, have you been making your goal achievement harder with your own fears or limiting beliefs? When you doubt your abilities and your success, you will find it harder to achieve your goals. Again, having the right thoughts and beliefs is important, so **be mindful of your thoughts**.

If you **believe you can**, but are **unsure** of **how**, remember the **3 steps to Overcoming All Obstacles.** You may be unsure of exactly how, but you will know at least one thing you can **try**. Then, you simply take the third step and **Take Action.** If you aren't successful, no big deal. Evaluate your results and go through the process again, and repeat as many times as needed. You are not failing. You are determining your process and path to success; your path may take 5, 15, or 150 more steps. And that's okay. It's your journey, not someone else's.

Is Goal Achievement really that simple?

Yes, it can be. Again, it can be as **easy or** as **hard** as you want to make it. Again, **You Can and Do decide** by your thoughts and beliefs. What can you do to ensure you reach your goal, your success? **Believe, take consistent actions,** and **be persistent** with your actions until you reach your goal.

SECRET

With belief, consistent action, and perseverance, you can accomplish any goal.

One daily action toward your goal is all it takes. **Isn't your success, your freedom, and your happiness worth that effort?** That is another captain obvious question. So, what are you waiting for? Decide on a goal and take action. Now! You deserve it.

Certified for Self-Use

Congratulations! You have now learned the **D.R.E.A.M. Goal-Setting and Goal-Achievement Method**. You now have a process or **system for success** that you can apply to any goal. Please remember what all the great philosophers, thinkers, and historical figures have said: that we become, or we are, or we act based on what we think about most. With that said, what are you thinking about the most? Is it your goal?

Buddha said, **"We are what we think. All that we are arises with our thoughts. With our thoughts, we make the world."**

Let's restate those beliefs/facts with **You** instead of we. Then it would read: **You are what you think. All that you are arises with your thoughts. With your thoughts, you make the world.**

Having this knowledge is like using fire. With fire, you can take plants or dead animals and **create** delicious meals. You can take clay and **make** plates, cups, and a wide variety of things. You can use it to melt and shape metal to **build** skyscrapers. And more basic, you can use it for **survival** by staying warm or to keep wild animals away. **Or** you can **burn down your house**, the forest, the World, and all the **living creatures** in it, including **yourself**.

You now have the knowledge to change the World, so what kind of World do you want to make? You can make it positive, negative, or random. Might I suggest you choose **a positive one**?

In summary, **your thoughts will make your world** whether you want them to or not, so choose them wisely.

Next, in Chapter 11, you will learn some techniques to help you build motivation, discipline, and habits that will also help you overcome obstacles and aide in your goal achievement.

> *The biggest and most difficult obstacle to reaching our goals is our own mind.*
>
> – Ron Carstens and a bunch of other smart people

> *Don't let the muggles get you down.*
>
> – J. K. Rowling

CHAPTER 11

Tips, Hacks, and Advanced Goal Planning

If you want one year of prosperity, grow seeds.
If you want ten years of prosperity, grow trees.
If you want a lifetime of wealth, grow your self-worth.

– Chinese Proverb

Have the courage to follow your heart and intuition.
They somehow already know what you truly want to become.

– Steve Jobs

TIPS AND HACKS

Where to Start?

For many people, the entire process of goal planning, goal
achievement, and all the thinking that goes into it is overwhelming.

Also, most people don't know where or how to begin, so they don't. As a fellow member of that group, I understand. No one told me how or where to start with my goals, so I focused on what was important to me, which was/is a typical response. People usually know what is important to them.

What Matters Most in Your Life?

When you ask people what the **most important things** are in **their lives**, their common answers are (not in any order):

- My family
- My job
- My faith
- My happiness
- My health

However, if you worked to improve only one of these things, like your relationship with your family, that does not mean your job or any of those other important things in your life would improve. Similarly, if you tried working on all of these different areas at the same time, you would probably not see much improvement for any of them.

The Common Denominator

No, you don't need to do any math here. You do need to see that the **common factor** in all the above responses is "My", which, of course, is **You. You are the common denominator.** So, if you want to improve all of the most important things in your life, you **start with improving yourself**. Improving and **bettering yourself improves all areas** of your life.

Yet, despite people knowing what they can do to improve themselves and their life, they don't do it. Unfortunately, others taught many of us to look outside of ourselves for answers, rather than to first look inside, to self-reflect, and help ourselves. So, we look around thinking some product, some shiny object we saw advertised is going to solve our problems, or that some stranger knows what is best for us. While those things are possible, most often the **answers we are searching for are usually inside of us.** They are things we can do for ourselves. Now, if you are seeking the help of a coach or mentor, that's different, and I encourage that help.

The main issue is a **lack of knowledge about our Self.** In order to master yourself and improve your goal-setting and goal-achievement, you **need** to **master Self-Awareness, Self-Worth, Self-Esteem**, and **Self-Confidence.** These things help you **build your I Can! attitude and belief.**

*** SECRET ***

When you master yourself, then you will have the Most Important Thing, you will Think and Believe: I CAN!

SELF-AWARENESS
perceiving and knowing
your thoughts, desires,
feelings, and motives

SELF-WORTH
accepting yourself as
you are and knowing
that you, matter and
have value

SELF

SELF-CONFIDENCE
your level of
belief in your
abilities

SELF-ESTEEM
the value you place
on yourself and
how you perceive
yourself

Self-Awareness

Self-awareness is **perceiving and knowing your thoughts, desires, feelings, and motives.** It's knowing and acknowledging your true self. When we **lack self-awareness**, we struggle with **goal setting** and **goal achievement.**

Many people just don't know what they really want. Not knowing and/or acknowledging one's true desires and thoughts causes people to accept their current situation and to stay in their comfort zone and not set goals, or at least not set very big goals. Even if you don't have very many or very big goals, being self-aware is to your benefit. Remember, in the Evaluate step, part of knowing where you are starting from is knowing yourself.

*** **SECRET** ***

Being honest with yourself can prevent you from wasting time, effort, or other resources on goals you are not fully committed to or that aren't part of your overall plan.

Self-Worth

Self-worth is **accepting yourself as you are** and knowing that you, as a person, matter and have value, regardless of your past, your present circumstances, or what others think of you..

Self-Esteem and Self-Confidence

Have you ever wondered why that nice, beautiful girl is with "that guy" who is not so nice or good-looking? Well, it's because he has self-confidence and self-esteem. He knows who he is and what he wants. He has strong beliefs about things and he's not afraid to say them.

Self-confidence is an important factor in achieving success in life. It can **help you make decisions, take goal-related risks, and face challenges.** Additionally, having a positive self-image can lead to **better mental and physical health**. It is said that **self-confidence is the best-looking suit/outfit you can wear.** Self-confidence is sexy, and people are attracted to it. Having a realistic and healthy sense of self-confidence is important, but if it becomes excessive, it can lead to overconfidence and poor decision-making.

Self-esteem is the **value you place on yourself** and how you perceive yourself. While similar, **Self-confidence** differs in that it is your level of **belief in your abilities**. Belief in oneself is important because it can affect one's self-esteem, motivation, and self-confidence in one's ability to achieve goals.

Ways to Improve Self-Awareness, Self-Worth, Self-Esteem, and Self-Confidence

Unfortunately, many people who struggle with low self-esteem and/or low self-confidence don't know how to improve it. These **techniques** will show you ways to build or help you improve your self-esteem and self-confidence and grow your self-awareness and self-worth.

1. **Set and accomplish small tasks/goals**: Start with small, manageable tasks and gradually work your way up to more challenging ones. This technique will help build a sense of accomplishment and your confidence.

2. **Practice self-care**: Taking care of your physical, emotional, and mental well-being can help improve self-esteem and self-confidence, and help you accomplish other goals.

3. **Learn from experience**: Reflect on past successes and failures and use them as opportunities to learn and grow.

4. **Be in a positive, caring environment**: Spending time with people who are supportive and encouraging can help build self-confidence and self-esteem, and avoid those people and situations that don't support you or who are negative.

5. **Surround yourself with positive role models**: Spend time with people who are successful and confident in their abilities. This time can serve as an inspiration and motivation to improve one's own self-confidence.

6. **Seek feedback**: Seek out feedback on your performance from others you trust. This step can help identify areas for improvement and provide a sense of progress.

7. **Positive self-talk**: Challenge negative thoughts and replace them with positive and realistic self-talk, like affirmations. **Affirmations** are positive statements about yourself and are a great way to build self-anything because you can make them about anything. Examples: I am a good person, I am smart, I am (state a positive). Besides building self-esteem or confidence, positive self-talk and affirmations also build resilience to negativity directed at you or around you.

8. **Practice Mindfulness**: Mindfulness practices such as meditation can help reduce stress and anxiety and can help build your self-belief.

9. **Confronting obstacles:** Confronting and overcoming fears and other obstacles can help build self-confidence by showing that you are capable of handling difficult situations.

10. **Practicing visualization**: Visualizing oneself successfully achieving a goal can help build self-confidence and motivation. Olympic and pro athletes and other top performers use this technique all the time.

11. **Engage in activities you enjoy**: Pursuing hobbies and interests can help build self-confidence by providing a sense of accomplishment and purpose. These types of activities also help you relax and reduce stress, which is part of self-care.

12. **Celebrate victories**: Reward yourself for your accomplishments. It doesn't have to be a big reward but try to make it meaningful to you. This type of positive reinforcement builds your self-confidence and motivation and leads to more success.

SECRET

When individuals believe in themselves and their abilities, they are more likely to take on challenges, persist in the face of setbacks, and ultimately achieve success.

For these reasons, improving your self-worth, self-esteem, and self-confidence is so important.

Motivation

Motivation is the **reason or driving force behind our actions**. It's what **pushes us to take action** and achieve goals. It helps us stay focused and determined to keep going when things get tough. And if we fail, it's what makes us try again.

Motivation can **come from internal or external sources**, such as coaches, mentors, friends, family, or even a role model. So, what motivates you? Why do you have the goals you have? **Write down your Whys to your goals.** Whatever your source of motivation may be, they are **essential tools** for success.

Your desire to achieve a goal usually starts with some type of motivation. You are tired of not having enough of something, or you desire something more. Most people can stay focused on achieving a goal for a few weeks, then, if you have taken no additional steps to keep yourself motivated, your focus and activities tend to decrease. Motivation is **temporary**, so it **needs** to be **renewed**.

Ways to Build Motivation

So **how can you stay motivated?** First, **know** that **you have achieved** many **goals and successes in the past**, so acknowledge your past achievements and experiences. In your **Goal Journal,** start a **list** of your past **experiences/achievements**. Even if you are relatively young, you have accomplished things, i.e. grades in school, diplomas, sports, meals you have cooked, anything you have created or completed, jobs that you wanted and got, people you met, compliments you received, or any type of award or recognition. Then, **add** to your **journal, daily or weekly**, and **review** your previous **accomplishments and add more goals**.

By remembering your past achievements and acknowledging new goals, you build self-esteem and confidence which in turn builds motivation. The **more self-esteem and confidence** you have, the **more likely you are to keep taking steps towards your goals**, especially if you feel those steps are getting harder or riskier. And by 'risky', I mean taking continued steps toward a bigger goal or stepping out of your comfort zone. Remember, the more risks you take, the more you will accomplish.

You can also **write** out the **reasons (your Whys)** you want to accomplish your goals in your **journal,** i.e., your **Motivation/ Why List**. Then **read out loud** your WHYs **daily,** along **with your goals**. Reviewing your Motivation List regularly helps you stay motivated and inspired to keep working toward your goal. Also, **write** out the **benefits** you are going to get **from** accomplishing **your goals** and read those. **Seeing, saying, and hearing your own words is Powerful!**

Another way to build **Motivation** is to **put** your **goal on** a **calendar** and **track** your **progress on** that **calendar**. Being able to see your progress daily is a conscious reminder of your goal, and it shows your successes, which also helps motivate you to keep going.

Finally, as explained in the previous section, you need to **celebrate your victories**. When you make your weekly goal, use small rewards as incentives to keep going.

Typically, **Motivation only lasts so long,** and then it usually decreases or stops altogether. And that is why you want to **build Discipline**.

Discipline

Discipline is the practice of **obeying rules** or a **code of behavior**. **Self-discipline** is the **ability to control one's thoughts, emotions, and behaviors** to achieve a goal or maintain self-regulation. It is also associated with the development of structure, self-control, and good habits. Building daily discipline can be a challenging task, but it is an important aspect of goal achievement.

However, the word Discipline is frequently viewed as a negative thing. People often view Discipline as **delayed gratification** because we stop doing something we like for a benefit that comes later, which most view as a negative. However, sometimes Discipline is really the **cost for prior gratification**. Often, when people must sacrifice something they enjoy doing, they tend to get their priorities and how they view the situation mixed up.

For example, I used to drink a certain cola in a red and white can. I thought it was the best drink ever invented. I drank one every day, sometimes two a day. However, after some severe stomach pain, a visit to an emergency clinic, and an irritable bowel syndrome diagnosis, I stopped drinking them. At first, I thought I was now sacrificing something I liked to drink in order to be healthy. Later, I realized that what I had actually done for years was sacrifice my health for an unhealthy drink, and the cost of my prior gratification came due. That cost was discipline today, of not drinking something

I liked, and being healthy instead. Remember, **self-discipline is Now, it's today.**

While **people** commonly **view discipline** as a **negative** thing, **its practice makes us better**, and it will **help you achieve** your goals. When you **understand** what **your focus** should be on, and **your Why**, like a Health goal, it **makes self-discipline easier** and helps you view it as something positive instead of something negative. It also helps you change those daily goals into habits much faster.

Techniques to Improve Discipline

Ways to improve discipline include the **same techniques to improve self-esteem, self-confidence, and Motivation.** Other **Discipline techniques** include:

1. **Start small,** with manageable tasks that are easy-to-accomplish tasks, and gradually increase the level of difficulty. This action will help you build momentum and create a sense of accomplishment.

2. **Create a schedule,** preferably a daily schedule, and stick to it as much as possible. Plan your day in advance and allocate specific time slots for different tasks and activities, like in your Action Plan.

3. **Learn time management and prioritization techniques** and apply them. Being more efficient with your time will help you accomplish more and help you find more free time. Do an internet search on these techniques, and you can easily learn about them.

4. **Make your Health a priority.** Improving your mental and physical health builds the Self, and those improvements will spread into your other goals and all areas of your life.

5. **Set clear goals** that clearly define what you want to accomplish. **Following the D.R.E.A.M. process** for goal setting and goal achievement will help you build discipline.

6. **Eliminate distractions** that prevent you from staying focused on your goals. This step may include turning off your phone, closing unnecessary tabs on your computer, or finding a quiet place to work.

7. **Hold yourself accountable** for your actions and keep track of your progress, like in the Monitor step. If you slip up, don't beat yourself up; instead, take it as a learning experience and move on.

8. **Reward yourself** for reaching your goals. It will help to make the process more enjoyable and will make the process more enjoyable and help keep you motivated, especially during the Monitor step.

9. **Reflect** on your progress regularly and evaluate what works and what doesn't. Make adjustments as needed and continue building your daily discipline. Again, like in the Monitor step.

10. **Be consistent** in your actions. **Consistency is key**. You build discipline over time. It's a long-term practice for the betterment of yourself and your goals, not a one-time event, so be consistent in your efforts and stick to your schedule and daily/weekly actions as much as possible.

Establish daily and **weekly routines** to build **consistency and persistency**, which will help **turn** them **into Habits**. While your past discipline helps you build upon today, your discipline yesterday only counts for yesterday. And you can't count on your intention of being disciplined tomorrow. It's **what you do today** that shows if you are being disciplined or not.

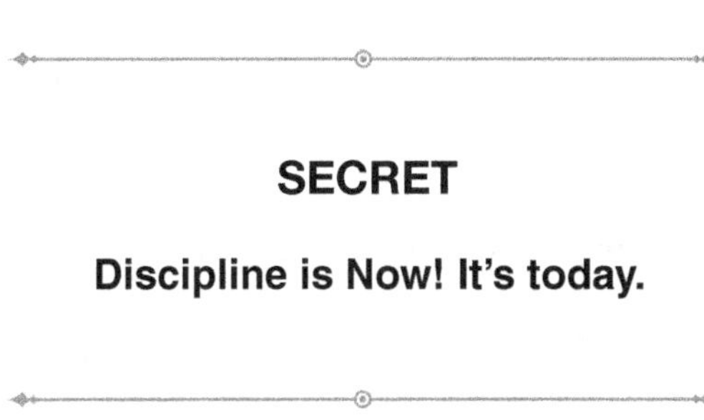

SECRET

Discipline is Now! It's today.

Note that building daily discipline requires time and effort, and may be difficult initially, but **consistent** effort and **perseverance** will **develop** it **into** a long-term **habit**.

Habits

Habits are **routine behaviors** that occur so regularly that they are often done **subconsciously**. They can be **positive or negative**, such as exercising regularly or smoking regularly. Often, habits form because of consistent reinforcement and can be difficult to change once established, so choose them wisely.

It typically takes 20 to 90 days to make or break a habit. The emotional intensity you have toward a habit and your frequency of doing, or not doing, the habit are the biggest factors in determining how long it will take you to form or break the habit.

We want our behaviors and goals, like making good eating choices and exercising, to become habits. **Establishing successful habits will help you accomplish your goals and dreams**.

How Do I Build Habits?

I'm glad you asked. You build habits using the **same techniques to build discipline** and by being **persistent** and **consistent** with your **actions/behaviors**. At a minimum, you need to perform your desired behavior for at least 20 days. Again, the frequency of the associated behavior and its emotional intensity are the biggest factors in determining how quickly the habit forms.

The **ideal process**/technique to **build a habit** is to:

- Use **motivation** to get you **started** down the **goal-achievement** path.

- Then **build self-discipline by establishing routines** for the activity/behavior that you want to make a habit.

- Finally, with **consistency** and **persistency of those daily activities/routines, they will become habits.**

If you are working on a goal that you want to be a habit, I suggest **setting** a **simultaneous goal** of doing the **desired behavior** for **at least 60 consecutive days,** or just add that part to your goal. Motivation can get some people through 20 to 30 days and then starts declining. Just look at all the New Year's resolutions that are dead before the end of January. By planning and achieving the goal of **60 days of consistency**, you will need to use some discipline-building techniques, which help lay the **foundation** for a **habit**. Also, with more time, the more likely you are to run into obstacles that you will have to overcome. Having to **adjust and overcome obstacles** is a real-world situation that you will face, and it is the **persistence** toward your goal that I refer to throughout this book.

This situation takes you through the whole **D.R.E.A.M. Method**, and you gain valuable experience and hopefully more confidence, which you can apply to future goals. Once you experience the positive results of achieving a few goals, then you should do some **Advanced Goal Planning**.

ADVANCED GOAL PLANNING

Advanced Goal Planning is simply more **conscious and long-term planning**, using time management and prioritization on a bigger and longer scale. You are **planning** and **coordinating** your **goals** over your **lifetime**, or at least a significant part of it, rather than just a few months or a year.

Why Do Advanced or Long-term Planning?

Great question! To help you **accomplish more goals** and have more **success**, more **freedom**, and more **happiness**, and to help you live the **life you want.** Also, long-term planning and goal coordination help you **maximize** your **resources.**

Hopefully, you have lots of goals and dreams. The younger you are, the more goals you should have. And the **sooner** you **start goal planning** and **taking action**, the **more** you will **achieve**. So why not **get started NOW?**

Also, finding your **life's purpose** and your **happiness** is more of **a journey**, not a quick trip to one destination. So be patient with yourself and keep exploring, by setting and achieving goals, until you find what connects and resonates with you. When your goals and values align, you'll feel a stronger **sense of purpose** and **fulfillment,** and that usually occurs over a longer period, not a short one.

Advanced Planning Techniques

There are several techniques you can use to maximize the effectiveness of your long-term goal planning and goal achievement.

Ideal Life Vision

The Ideal Life Vision technique is like the Goal Discovery technique in Chapter 5, where you **design your ideal day**, week, month, or year. However, instead of designing one day, you design your **ideal life.** I know that's not something most people think about, at least not in a very detailed way, but **how can you expect to live your ideal life if you don't think about it and plan for it?** The answer is you can't unless your ideal life is letting life give you random results. If you want to live your ideal life, you need to think about it and plan for it because **your ideal life is possible.** This premise goes for all of your goals.

Have you thought about what your ideal life looks like? What is your ideal or dream job? Do you go into an office, work from home, or work wherever you want using your phone or laptop? Where do you live? Describe your ideal house. What kind of car do you drive? What do you do for fun? Who lives with you? Describe your business or career plans, your personal and family life, your desired daily activities, and any other goals you want to achieve.

Take your **ideal day** description of the life you want, and then **extend** your plan out to **a year**, and include as many goals and Goal Categories as you can, and write them out, describing all the things you want to have, be, do, and achieve. **Then,** extend your plan out to **five years**, then **ten**, and **so on**. Next, you will make Action Plans for your goals due in the coming year. Then repeat, yearly or every few years as needed. Yes, long-term planning can take significant effort, but isn't your ideal life worth it? Or you can wait and see if your ideal life happens by chance.

I realize a younger person may find this approach not very practical or maybe too overwhelming in that five or ten years out is too far in the future for them to reasonably plan for, and that's okay. Just plan as far as you can. And the more details you include, the better. The **more you plan, the better**, as **you** are **more likely**

to achieve planned goals than unplanned ones. Creating this ideal vision of your life will give you more direction and motivation. Another result of Advanced Planning is you will get better at goal setting and goal achievement as experience helps.

The Rocking Chair Method

Another Advanced Planning technique is the Rocking Chair method, where you start at the end of your life and plan backward. Imagine that you are 100 years old, sitting in your rocking chair. **Yes, 100!** It's possible, and if you plan for it, then it's probable. Now, **describe** to someone **all** the things/**goals** that you would have **achieved or done in your life,** and make a **list** of **those goals.** Then, take your list of goals and **make Action Plans** for them. Yes, you may end up with a bunch of big Action Plans. Hopefully so, but **thinking, planning,** and **doing** is how **you make** your **desired life** happen.

Also, the more specific you get about your life vision and goals, the better. **Specific details** and **thoughts elicit more emotion,** and it's this **emotion** that **motivates people** to act. **Emotions** also **get** the **subconscious to start working** toward your goals. Again, when your goals align with your values, you will feel a greater sense of purpose, personal growth, and fulfillment.

Advanced Planning should cover all, or at least most, of the goal categories listed in Chapter 5. Reviewing the goal categories and the various goals within each will help when planning. Just as a refresher, those **Goal Categories are: Health, Career, Financial, Social, Spirituality, and Personal Growth.**

When Should You Start Planning?

Now! Or **ASAP!** You should start planning as soon as possible. And it doesn't matter how old you are because **it's never too late**

to Plan and to Do. However, the sooner you start, the better, and the more time, money, and other resources you will save. Remember, **my lack of planning and a detailed goal cost me over $220,000 and almost three years**. Don't let that happen to you. **Start Now!**

Ideally, and practically, I recommend you start planning **when you start high school**. In most high schools, you can start taking elective classes that relate to various careers. Also, you can take **dual credit classes** that give you college credits in classes like English, History, Math, and Computer Science. You can graduate from high school with an associate degree, which is approximately two years' worth of college credits. That early **planning** is easily **worth $30,000, or more,** for the college credits and **saves you two years of time**. Those two years spent at a full-time job instead of school are **worth ever more money**. Isn't two years of income worth you doing a little planning? Yes, another Captain Obvious question.

Also, in high school, people turn 15 and 16, and can start working or doing internships at companies, which can lead to future jobs or careers. While you can legally start working at age 14, there are certain rules that apply, and most US companies have a minimum age of 16 years old to work. I started working at age 15 and bought my first car in high school, and that proud **feeling of accomplishment** is something that I still feel today.

I know you are saying, "Ron, it's a little late, since I'm not in high school anymore." I get it. However, you can pass this knowledge on to someone else or apply it to your kids for their college, which can still **save you money**.

How to Start Advanced Planning

If you used one of the Advanced Planning techniques, then review all your goals with a focus on the most important ones. Also, look for connections between your goals, like time frames and goal categories, so that there is coordination between your goals. Next, start developing short-, mid-, and long-term Action Plans. The more related goals you can do this type of long-term planning with, the better, as you will accomplish more goals and save time, money, and other resources.

Small Steps

Most people think it takes some big effort to make a plan and to make changes in their lives, which is why they procrastinate or let some other obstacle stop them. They make a New Year's resolution but stop working on it a few weeks later. However, you can start working on a goal with very little effort.

You can **start** by **taking** a few **small steps**, like just walking to the corner or your street, then walking around the block, and then walking around two blocks, and so on. Or reading/learning one page a day. Then, reading/learning two pages a day or cutting back on one soda or fancy coffee a day, then two days, and so on.

Some people don't want to write their goals down which is okay, so don't let the idea of having to have a plan stop you from starting toward a goal. You **can start** these small steps and build on them **without having a plan in place**.

However, once you get started and **when** you have a clearly thought-out **goal in mind**, you should **write it down**, as that is **part of the goal-setting and goal-achievement process**. It can be one sheet of paper with your goal and a list of the needed steps/actions. It does not have to be complicated. Then, write down your other goals and see how you can integrate them into long-term plans.

THREE ULTIMATE HACKS

Write Your Goals Down

In short, and repeated because of importance, **writing your goal down gives you the biggest increase in your chance of success at your goal.** You are taking the invisible and bringing it into the physical world. Also, you want that goal to be "official." Writing your goal down makes it official and makes your intention to achieve that goal clear to your mind and the Universe.

Get a Coach/Mentor/Advisor

After writing your goals down, **having a coach or mentor provides the next biggest increase in your chance of achieving your goal. You can further increase your chances by having a coach or mentor who was successful in the same area as your goal.**

If you still haven't met with a coach or mentor regarding your goals, I suggest you do so. Remember the Introduction to this book, if I, or some other **coach/mentor, can save you time and money**, wouldn't you want to know what we had to say? If you get the results you want, those coaches, advisors, and mentors will easily pay for themselves. Also, you can't do everything by yourself, and you are probably not an expert on every goal you have, so don't try to do it all. Be smart and use coaches, mentors, and advisors to help you plan and achieve your goals.

Most millionaires, or people our society considers successful, have a coach or mentor of some type. Also, most millionaires have help. They know they can't do everything themselves, so they have people helping them. They have a team. Yes, you can be successful without being a millionaire or having help. The point is that seeking and getting help is a smart thing to do.

Be Persistent

Persistence is a **characteristic of successful people**, so if you want to succeed, keep working toward your goal no matter what. If you haven't quit, then you haven't failed. Keep going. Ruben Gonzalez qualified for the Olympics in less than four years in a sport he had never done before, and then qualified for three more Olympics in one of the toughest events. He was 47 years old at his last Olympics, and at 55, he became the oldest person ever to compete internationally in luge. He never won the gold medal, but he achieved his goals. And **he is an Olympian forever!**

At this point, you should know how to **develop** and **set goals** and **make** and follow your **Action Plan**. The **next step** is for You to **DO it! Not tomorrow, not next week- NOW!**

You are never too old to set another goal
or to dream a new dream.

– Les Brown

CHAPTER 12

25 Secrets to Success and Finding Resources

*Every great dream begins with a dreamer. Always
remember, you have within you the strength, the patience,
and the passion to reach for the stars to change the world.*

– Author Unknown

Most of these **secrets to success** were highlighted in the
previous chapters, but a few were not. In case you missed
them, I have restated and/or summarized them here, mostly in the
order as they appear in the book except for **Secret #1** which is **the
Most Important Thing**.

Secret #1

For your success, the Absolute, Most Important Thing You Must Do
is YOU MUST THINK and BELIEVE: **I CAN!**

Secret #2

You can change your results in life, and you CAN choose to have better results and a better life.

Secret #3

You should set goals because life happens to you whether you want it to or not, and you will continue to get more results whether you want them or not.

Secret #4

By setting goals and taking action to reach them, YOU get to decide the outcomes of your life rather than life deciding for you, and you get better results.

Secret #5

You should begin your goal journey by educating yourself, and learning should be a lifelong goal.

Secret #6

Your success will be determined by your self-belief and your actions.

Secret #7

Simply by writing down your goal, you significantly improve your chances of achieving that goal.

Secret #8

The more often you take action on a goal and the more important that goal is to you, the faster you can turn that goal into a habit.

Secret #9

Your Health is the most important goal category as its benefits give you the biggest help overall and is a catalyst for success with your other goals.

Secret #10

In terms of increasing your odds of achieving your goal, after simply writing down your goal, having a coach or mentor provides the biggest increase in your chance of achieving your goal.

Secret #11

The biggest and most difficult obstacles to achieving any of our goals are our own limiting beliefs.

Secret #12

If you want to be successful, you must take ownership of your thoughts, actions, and situation.

Secret #13

Advice from coaches and mentors on how to plan for, avoid, or handle an Obstacle can be invaluable.

Secret #14

With belief, consistent action, and perseverance, you can accomplish any goal.

Secret #15

When you master yourself, you will have the Most Important Thing: you will Think and Believe—**I CAN!**

Secret #16

Being honest with yourself can prevent you from wasting time, effort, or other resources on goals you are not fully committed to or that aren't part of your overall plan.

Secret #17

When individuals believe in themselves and their abilities, they are more likely to take on challenges, persist in the face of setbacks, and ultimately achieve success.

Secret #18

Discipline is Now! It's today.

Secret #19

You destroy and Overcome Obstacles by taking action.

Secret #20

Successful people believe in themselves. They did not let their current circumstances, race, social status, financial status, or any other circumstance limit them.

Secret #21

The goals you want to achieve and your journey to them are uniquely yours. And that's why You Can't Copy Someone Else's homework. You have to do your own work!

Secret #22

Understand that others' judgments of you are often a reflection of their own insecurities.

Secret #23

Having a specific goal or definite purpose gives you more desire, and more desire leads to more action.

Secret #24

The self-development books, programs, or systems that motivate you to take action are the best.

Secret #25

If you want to live your ideal life, you need to think about it and plan for it. Your "dream" life is possible.

More on Resources

This section is to assist you in locating various resources, so they can help you with your specific goals that you discovered or realized in **Step 2 of the D.R.E.A.M. process, Resources.** Also, I wanted to repeat and emphasize the **importance** of these **Resources,** especially coaches, mentors, and other experts.

Remember, **Coaches, Mentors, and other experts can provide the biggest increases to your success,** so look for ones who can advise you for the specific goal you are working on. You will find examples of specific coaches, mentors, and experts under their respective goal categories that follow. One type of professional that can assist you with goal planning and goal achievement is a **Life Coach.**

Life Coaches

Life coaches **help people make goals and guide them** toward achieving those goals. They should be able to help you plan for goals in all the goal categories and integrate multiple goals when doing long-term planning. They can also be a **support person**. While a good friend may be a good support person, a friend may also be more lenient with you and may not be straightforward with you when they should because they don't want to hurt your feelings. At the same time, a life coach will probably be more upfront or matter-of-fact about something, which is what you need.

Life Coaches should also be able to direct you to or help you **find the right coach** or mentor for **help** with more **specific goals**, like a Health goal of getting stronger, or training for a specific sport or competition. For specific goals, like these, you may need or should get an expert like a personal trainer. Another example would be talking with a Financial Advisor about retirement plans and other financial goals.

My **life coach, Allison**, specializes in Goal Setting, Work-Life Balance, Time Management, Conflict Resolution, Team and Strategy Building, Parenting Issues, Career Building, and Whole Life Strategy. She was life coaching before it was even called life coaching. While she tends to focus on work-life balance for people, with her wide variety of experience, she **can help** you with goal setting and planning in **all** the **goal categories.**

Also, she, like many life coaches, works with clients **by phone, video calls, or in person,** if you live in the area. You can find a direct link to her website and other **Resources** on my website **icandream.net**.

A quick **internet search** for **"life coaches in my area"** will provide you with a list of potential coaches. Like anything else, I suggest you research potential coaches by reviewing their websites and other social media to learn about them, to find the one that best matches you and your needs.

FINDING RESOURCES

For anyone who is unaware or unsure of the Resources available to you for any goal, you can do an **internet search** on **"resources for ___(state your goal)."** Yes, it's that easy. You can **add other words to clarify or specify** what you are looking for, for example, **"natural** resources for..." or **"free** resources for weight loss."

Other helpful words/phrases to aid in your searches are:

- **Best** resources for...

- **Expert** resources for...

- **Top 10** resources for...

- **Free** resources for...
- **Local** resources for...
- (Your goal) ...**for beginners/experts/men/women/kids/ other identifiers**
- **Websites** for (your goal)

In the **Goal Categories** below, under **Possible Resources,** I've listed **various professionals** associated with that category that can help you with your related goals and a few **example internet searches**. Note, there are more professionals associated with each area. These lists are just some of the most common persons/professionals.

Health

Exercise, Diet, Sleep, Relaxation, Hygiene
Possible Resources

- Exercise—Fitness Coaches, Personal Trainers
- Diet—Nutritionist, Nutrition Coaches
- All—Health Coaches, Wellness Coaches

Example internet searches

- Local Fitness Coaches
- Personal Trainers Near Me, Or Personal Trainers In . . . (Your City, State, Etc.)
- Personal Trainer For (Your Sport)

Career/Occupation

The best resource would be **someone** who is already doing/working **in the particular occupation** of your interest. If you don't know anyone, then I would do an internet search for that occupation/job adding "near me." Then you read about them and possibly call or email them with any specific questions. Yes, you can call or email a stranger. Again, you may be surprised at how many people are willing to help.

Possible Resources

- Persons already in that specific job
- School counselors
- Teachers or professors of that specific profession or occupation

Internet search for

- **local _______ (fill in the blank with your job/occupation)**
- **top 10 _______ in (your state)**

Financial/Lifestyle

This category includes too many areas and possible goals to cover, so only a few common resources are listed. For anyone who is unaware or unsure of Resources available to you in any category, or just wants additional information, do an **internet search on "resources for _____(state your goal).** Example: "Resources for retirement planning."

Possible Resources

- Tax accountants

- Tax and estate planning attorneys
- Financial advisors
- Local bankers
- Successful friends
- Other professionals specific to your goal, like a realtor

A Financial Advisor, like my friend Darren, can provide you with expert advice on retirement plans, small business planning, and other financial/lifestyle goals. You can find a direct link to him and other Resources on my website **icandream.net**.

Social

Sometimes pride gets in our way, but for Social questions, I would start with your friends and/or family. While their advice may not be objective, they know you, and their advice should have more insight because of that familiarity with you and your situation.

Possible Resources

- Psychologists and psychiatrists
- Therapists
- Various types of counselors i.e., relationship, marriage
- Religious leaders
- Teachers, professors

Spirituality/Religion

This category is another one that can be very personal, where pride or fears of embarrassment might stop someone from asking for help.

To those with concerns, I assure you, you are not the first person with these concerns. Most professionals are aware of these issues and should be able to ease your concerns.

Possible Resources

- Spiritual or religious leaders for that particular practice/faith
- Teachers, professors
- Books
- The internet

For possible Resources available, do an **internet search on "resources available for __(state your goal)**.

Personal Growth

If you are an older person, chances are, you're already aware of resources available to you for your Personal Growth journey. For anyone who is unaware or unsure of the Resources available to you in this category, or any category, or just wants additional information, do an internet search on "resources for . . . (state your goal).

Since the **Personal Growth** category can include any goal, your **Resources can be anyone or anything** previously mentioned.

No Conclusion:
A Call to Action

The **D.R.E.A.M. Goal-Setting and Goal-Achievement Method** is a **system for success.** It shows you how to develop and set goals, how to make an action plan to follow to achieve those goals, how to monitor your progress, and make adjustments to your plans if needed.

Your **I CAN! mindset** and **belief in yourself** are the **most important messages** in this book or any self-improvement book or program. It is the **starting point for any goal** and success. You can have more success, freedom, and happiness, and live the life you want. All you need to do is choose that life, follow the **D.R.E.A.M. Method**, and **take action**. You taking action is how you **transform** your life.

A quote commonly attributed to Mother Teresa, but the author is unknown, says, **"I alone cannot change the world, but I can cast a stone across waters to create many ripples."** I'm glad the author is unknown because I wouldn't want to say Mother Teresa was wrong. But she helped thousands of people during her life, and she was an inspiration to millions, if not billions of people. **She did change the World through her actions.**

I created a **new goal-setting** and **goal-achievement method** to **make the World a better place** by **helping others** achieve their goals and dreams. This book is my stone across the waters which I threw to you. It's now in your hands, and **you decide** the size of your ripple. However, I am asking you to **please continue making positive ripples**, and let's **change the World.**

You are the **designer**, the **builder**, the **artist**, and **creator of your life**, your future, and the **World** you live in. You are creating it right now and getting either planned or random results. **You control your future.** If **you act** on your goals and dreams, you **can change your life** and the **World.** So, what are you going to create? **What are you going to DO? It's up to You!**

And **congratulations on** any and all of **your** future **goal achievements! I know YOU CAN!**

References

Canfield, J., & Switzer, J. (2015). Table of Contents. In *The Success Principles* (10th ed., pp. xv–xvii). essay, HarperCollins.

Covey, S. R. (2020). Table of Contents. In *The 7 Habits of Highly Effective People* (25th Anniversary Edition, pp. xv–xvi). essay, Simon and Schuster.

Doran, G. T. (1981). "There's a S.M.A.R.T. way to write management goals and objectives." *Management Review*.

Eveleth, R. (2013, May 17). "Two-Thirds of the World Still Hate Lefties." Smithsonian.com. https://www.smithsonianmag.com/smart-news/two-thirds-of-the-world-still-hates-lefties-64727388/

Ford, H., & Crowther, S. (2024). *My life and work*. Duke Classics.

Gardner, S., & Albee, D. (2015, February 1). "Study focuses on strategies for achieving goals, resolutions." *Dominican Scholar*. https://scholar.dominican.edu/news-releases/266

Gillaspie, D. (2017, January 20). "You'll Never Accomplish Goals You Don't Really Care About." *Entrepreneur*. https://www.entrepreneur.com/living/youll-never-accomplish-goals-you-dont-really-care-about/254371

Gonzalez, R. O. (2014*). The Courage to succeed. Success Secrets of an Unlikely Four-Time Olympian*. Olympic Motivation.

Kohl, D. (2024, January 18). "Goal setting 101: Control variables in farm business." FarmProgress.com. http://FarmProgress.com

Appendix

Goals Lists
Experience List
Interests List
Why/Motivation List
Resources List
Action Plan
Habit Tracker

For these forms and other downloadable forms, go to icandream.net, under Resources.

YOUR GOALS LIST

1. _______________________________________
2. _______________________________________
3. _______________________________________
4. _______________________________________
5. _______________________________________
6. _______________________________________
7. _______________________________________
8. _______________________________________
9. _______________________________________
10. _______________________________________
11. _______________________________________
12. _______________________________________
13. _______________________________________
14. _______________________________________
15. _______________________________________
16. _______________________________________
17. _______________________________________
18. _______________________________________
19. _______________________________________
20. _______________________________________

YOUR GOALS
WHAT DO YOU WANT TO BE?

1. ____
2. ____
3. ____
4. ____
5. ____
6. ____
7. ____
8. ____
9. ____
10. ____
11. ____
12 ____
13. ____
14. ____
15. ____
16. ____
17. ____
18. ____
19. ____
20. ____

YOUR GOALS
WHAT DO YOU WANT TO HAVE?

[171]

1. ____

2. ____

3. ____

4. ____

5. ____

6. ____

7. ____

8. ____

9. ____

10. ____

11. ____

12 ____

13. ____

14. ____

15. ____

16. ____

17. ____

18. ____

19. ____

20. ____

YOUR GOALS
WHAT DO YOU WANT TO DO?

1. ____

2. ____

3. ____

4. ____

5. ____

6. ____

7. ____

8. ____

9. ____

10. ____

11. ____

12. ____

13. ____

14. ____

15. ____

16. ____

17. ____

18. ____

19. ____

20. ____

YOUR GOALS
WHAT DO YOU WANT TO ACHIEVE?

1. ____

2. ____

3. ____

4. ____

5. ____

6. ____

7. ____

8. ____

9. ____

10. ____

11. ____

12. ____

13. ____

14. ____

15. ____

16. ____

17. ____

18. ____

19. ____

20. ____

YOUR EXPERIENCE LIST

1. ____
2. ____
3. ____
4. ____
5. ____
6. ____
7. ____
8. ____
9. ____
10. ____
11. ____
12. ____
13. ____
14. ____
15. ____
16. ____
17. ____
18. ____
19. ____
20. ____

YOUR INTERESTS LIST

1. ____

2. ____

3. ____

4. ____

5. ____

6. ____

7. ____

8. ____

9. ____

10. _______________________________________

11. _______________________________________

12 ____

13. _______________________________________

14. _______________________________________

15. _______________________________________

16. _______________________________________

17. _______________________________________

18. _______________________________________

19. _______________________________________

20. _______________________________________

YOUR WHY/MOTIVATION LIST

1. ____

2. ____

3. ____

4. ____

5. ____

6. ____

7. ____

8. ____

9. ____

10. ____

11. ____

12. ____

13. ____

14. ____

15. ____

16. ____

17. ____

18. ____

19. ____

20. ____

RESOURCES LIST

Resources You Have: **Resources You Need:**

ACTION PLAN

Goal:____

Day:__ Week:__ Month:__　　　　**Time(s)**　　　　**Completed**

Action 1:_______________________　__________　__________

Action 2:_______________________　__________　__________

Action 3:_______________________　__________　__________

Action 4:_______________________　__________　__________

Action 5:_______________________　__________　__________

Day:__ Week:__ Month:__　　　　**Time(s)**　　　　**Completed**

Action 1:_______________________　__________　__________

Action 2:_______________________　__________　__________

Action 3:_______________________　__________　__________

Action 4:_______________________　__________　__________

Action 5:_______________________　__________　__________

Day:__ Week:__ Month:__　　　　**Time(s)**　　　　**Completed**

Action 1:_______________________　__________　__________

Action 2:_______________________　__________　__________

Action 3:_______________________　__________　__________

Action 4:_______________________　__________　__________

Action 5:_______________________　__________　__________

Day:__ Week:__ Month:__   **Time(s)**   **Completed**

Action 1:______________________   __________   __________

Action 2:______________________   __________   __________

Action 3:______________________   __________   __________

Action 4:______________________   __________   __________

Action 5:______________________   __________   __________

Day:__ Week:__ Month:__   **Time(s)**   **Completed**

Action 1:______________________   __________   __________

Action 2:______________________   __________   __________

Action 3:______________________   __________   __________

Action 4:______________________   __________   __________

Action 5:______________________   __________   __________

Day:__ Week:__ Month:__   **Time(s)**   **Completed**

Action 1:______________________   __________   __________

Action 2:______________________   __________   __________

Action 3:______________________   __________   __________

Action 4:______________________   __________   __________

Action 5:______________________   __________   __________

7th Day or at least **1 day**, **take a break**. If you had a successful week, then reward yourself w/ something like, extra TV time, a dessert, a "cheat" meal, a weekend getaway.

Monitor: Measurements/results/completed activities used to determine your progress toward your goal.

Day/Week/Month 1:
Day/Week/Month 2:
Day/Week/Month 3:
Day/Week/Month 4:

HABIT TRACKER

Habit: ______________________________ :
Starting # of Successful Days: ______________

Habit: ______________________________ :
Starting # of Successful Days: ______________

Habit: ______________________________ :
Starting # of Successful Days: ______________

MOTIVATION-WHY

Why do you have these particular goals? Who are your goals for? What are the outcomes do you want?

1.

2.

3.

4.

Acknowledgements

To Mom, Dad, Jack, Luke, Lois Gibson, Jack Canfield, Patty Aubery, Shannon Hazel, Ricky Rojas, Troy Smith, Allison Goldberg, Darren McNeely, Olive McCrary, Doug Hoffschwelle, and Ruben Gonzalez.

Thank you all for your encouragement, support, and advice in helping me finish this book. Your help was invaluable, and I appreciate each of you so much.

About the Author

Ron Carstens is an author, entrepreneur, business consultant, and life-long learner, who has spent his life helping and educating people. Ron served in the military and government before changing careers to the financial industry. As a financial advisor for a large national bank, he helped individuals and small business owners plan and achieve their various financial and business goals. Then, September 11, 2001, occurred, which shattered the financial world along with Ron's new career. In the wake of 9/11, he faced tremendous obstacles of customers' financial fears, pressure from management for new sales, and acting in customer's best interest while keeping his integrity with a job where his income was 100% sales commission based. After evaluating his new circumstances, Ron chose to keep his integrity and went back to his government job.

Ron continued his self-improvement education and explored entrepreneurship starting several of his own businesses. Throughout his various changes and challenges, Ron observed many people experiencing the same problems he had encountered. People had goals, but they didn't know how to get started or the best way to achieve them. They were not taught about goal setting or action plans despite their importance and impact they can have on our lives. Also, the amount of information on goals can be overwhelming, often contradictory and confusing. To solve these problems and give people proper guidance, Ron took his 35-plus years of experience, education and training in personal growth/self-improvement, goals, leadership, management, team building and training and created the D.R.E.A.M. Goal-Setting and Goal-Achievement Method. Based on the best and proven techniques, Ron now shares his new system for success to help people reach their goals and live a better life. Currently, Ron lives in Houston, Texas, with his two sons, a cat and a bird.

www.icandream.net

www.ingramcontent.com/pod-product-compliance
Lightning Source LLC
Chambersburg PA
CBHW070858160726
48004CB00003B/1132